The Way to Make Money: Mastering the Psychology of Wealth and Success

PUBLISHED BY Logan Sharpe

Table of contents

Nessuna voce di sommario trovata.

Introduction

"The curious paradox is that when I accept myself just as I am, then I can change." These words from Carl Rogers capture a truth that extends far beyond personal growth or therapy. They speak directly to how we handle money. For most of us, financial behavior is not simply a matter of arithmetic or following a set of neatly defined steps outlined in financial advice columns. If it were, the path to wealth would be straightforward. We would spend less than we earn, invest wisely, avoid unnecessary debt, and secure our future with disciplined savings. Yet, the reality is strikingly different. Millions of people, regardless of their income level or access to information, struggle with money management, repeat destructive financial patterns, and find themselves unable to achieve the stability and freedom they long for. The paradox lies in recognizing that financial transformation does not begin with more external advice or stricter rules but with an acceptance of how we think, feel, and act in relation to money.

Traditional financial advice often fails because it assumes human beings are perfectly rational actors. It treats us as if we were machines capable of digesting facts, calculating probabilities, and executing strategies without hesitation or deviation. The reality, however, is that we are emotional creatures shaped by our upbringing, our experiences, and the cultural messages that surround us. Money is not just numbers on a spreadsheet—it is loaded with meaning. It is tied to our sense of security, our identity, our aspirations, and our fears. Each decision we make, whether to spend impulsively, to avoid investing out of fear, or to give generously beyond our means, carries the imprint of psychological forces often hidden beneath the surface. Without understanding these forces, even the most carefully crafted financial plan is likely to collapse.

The gap between what we know and what we do with money is one of the defining challenges of modern life. Nearly everyone is aware that saving for the future is wise, that high-interest debt is harmful, and that reckless spending leads to regret. Yet awareness alone does not translate into action. This gap is not due to ignorance but to the invisible scripts that govern our financial choices. These scripts are formed early in life, often before we are conscious of them, through observing how our parents handled money, through the values our culture attached to wealth, and through the emotional imprints of success and failure. A child who sees financial conflict in the home may grow into an adult who avoids money conversations altogether. Someone who experienced scarcity may hoard cash compulsively even when it prevents them from enjoying life. Another who was rewarded with gifts or indulgences may associate money with love and thus struggle to say no to unnecessary spending.

This book is not another manual filled with formulas and prescriptive advice detached from real human experience. It is about bridging the worlds of psychology and finance to show how lasting wealth begins not with external strategies but with internal awareness. By understanding the hidden beliefs that shape our financial behavior, we can begin to rewire our relationship with money. Once this shift occurs, the practical tools—budgeting, investing, building passive income, managing debt—finally make sense and stick, because they are no longer imposed rules but natural extensions of a healthier mindset.

Consider how many times people resolve to change their financial habits with the best intentions. They create a strict budget, download an app to track expenses, or vow to stop using credit cards. At first, enthusiasm carries them forward. But soon, old patterns resurface. Emotional triggers—stress, boredom, envy, or even celebration—lead to impulsive spending or avoidance. The cycle repeats, leaving them more discouraged than before. The problem is not a lack of willpower; it is that the deeper psychological patterns have not been addressed. Just as dieting often fails because it ignores the emotional relationship people have with food, so too does financial advice fail when it ignores the emotional and psychological relationship people have with money.

Accepting ourselves as we are, as Rogers suggests, is the starting point. When we acknowledge that our financial habits are rooted in something deeper than numbers, we open the door to change. We no longer blame ourselves for being "bad with money" or label our struggles as personal failings. Instead, we approach them with curiosity and compassion. We ask, "Why do I react this way? What story am I carrying about money? Whose voice echoes in my financial decisions?" From there, new possibilities emerge. Change becomes less about forcing behavior and more about transforming the foundation on which those behaviors rest.

This approach is especially crucial today. We live in an age of constant comparison, where social media parades images of luxury, success, and lifestyle upgrades that often mask hidden debts and financial stress. We are bombarded with marketing messages designed to tap into our insecurities and desires. Easy credit makes it possible to live beyond our means with little immediate consequence. At the same time, financial products have grown more complex, from cryptocurrencies to investment derivatives, leaving many feeling overwhelmed or excluded. In such an environment, merely telling people to "spend wisely" or "invest early" rings hollow. What is needed is a deeper recalibration of how we think about money and how we make decisions in the face of psychological and cultural pressures.

Throughout this book, we will explore why traditional advice is insufficient and how a psychological approach can lead to lasting transformation. We will examine the unconscious money scripts we inherit and how they manifest in adulthood. We will look at the role of emotions—fear, guilt, pride, and hope—in driving financial behavior. We will consider how cultural narratives around success and wealth shape our expectations and limits. We will explore the neuroscience of scarcity and abundance, showing how our brains are wired to react to financial stress in ways that can sabotage long-term planning. We will uncover how cognitive biases cloud our judgment and lead to costly mistakes, and how awareness can free us from their grip.

But this is not just an exploration of theory. The goal is to offer a bridge from understanding to action. Practical steps will accompany the insights, but always in a way that respects the psychological reality of human behavior. For example, we will see why automating savings works not because people lack intelligence but because it bypasses the constant negotiation with temptation. We will examine why creating multiple income streams is not just a financial strategy but a psychological buffer against fear and scarcity. We will learn why generosity, far from being a luxury, is often a key to unlocking financial confidence and abundance.

The promise of this book is simple: by aligning mindset with practical action, lasting wealth becomes possible. Wealth here does not mean only material abundance but also peace of mind, resilience in the face of setbacks, and the freedom to pursue a life aligned with one's values. Money is not an end in itself but a tool, and how we wield it depends less on external circumstances than on the internal stories we tell ourselves.

As you read, you may find echoes of your own journey. You may recognize patterns inherited from your family, cultural pressures that shape your decisions, or emotions that have silently driven your financial life. You may also find hope in realizing that these patterns are not destiny. Just as we once learned them, we can unlearn or reshape them. The paradox Rogers describes—that change begins with acceptance—will guide us throughout. By accepting ourselves and our financial history without judgment, we gain the power to step into a new future.

The path ahead is not about quick fixes or miracle solutions. It is about cultivating a new way of seeing, one that honors both the rational and the emotional dimensions of money. It is about replacing shame with understanding, fear with awareness, and confusion with clarity. When these shifts occur, the practical strategies that once felt impossible begin to feel natural, and financial progress becomes not a battle but a byproduct of alignment.

This is the journey we are about to take together. It is a journey into the psychology of money, into the hidden forces that shape our reality, and into the practices that can lead not just to wealth, but to a healthier, freer, and more intentional life.

Chapter 1: The **Wealth** Mindset Matrix

Research from Harvard Business School reveals a startling truth: 95 percent of lottery winners return to their previous financial status within five years, while self-made millionaires who lose everything often rebuild their fortunes within three to five years. This data highlights a crucial reality—wealth is not primarily about the amount of money one acquires but about the mindset one carries. The difference between fleeting riches and sustainable prosperity lies in the psychological frameworks we inherit, absorb, and reinforce over a lifetime. To understand why so many people remain trapped in cycles of financial struggle despite having access to advice and opportunities, we must first examine the hidden architecture of what psychologists call "money scripts." These are the unconscious beliefs that shape how we view money, how we use it, and ultimately how we limit or expand our financial potential.

1.1 Deconstructing Money Scripts

The idea of money scripts is rooted in the understanding that financial behavior is rarely a matter of pure logic. Beneath every decision—whether to save, spend, invest, or give—lie layers of meaning and belief that have often been formed long before adulthood. By deconstructing these scripts, we uncover the psychological forces that explain why people consistently act in ways that seem contrary to their best interests, why wealth slips through some hands like water, and why others rebuild it again and again. Three core elements of these scripts deserve close attention: inherited beliefs, cultural programming, and emotional anchoring.

Inherited Beliefs

From the earliest years of childhood, money is present in ways that are subtle yet powerful. A child does not need to understand the mechanics of a mortgage or the intricacies of investment accounts to absorb a family's financial atmosphere. Every argument about bills, every celebration over a tax refund, every act of generosity or miserliness becomes part of a silent curriculum. Children watch how their parents handle money—whether they discuss it openly, treat it as a source of stress, or avoid the topic altogether—and these observations lay the groundwork for unconscious blueprints that persist into adulthood.

For example, a child raised in a household where money was scarce may internalize the belief that financial security is always tenuous, no matter how much is earned. This individual may grow up to hoard cash compulsively, refusing to spend even on necessary items, or may swing to the opposite extreme, spending recklessly in an attempt to escape the fear of scarcity. Conversely, a child from an affluent household where money flowed freely might absorb the notion that wealth is inexhaustible, only to face disillusionment later in life when reality does not match the expectation. These patterns often emerge not from explicit teachings but from observation and emotional osmosis.

What makes inherited beliefs so enduring is that they operate beneath conscious awareness. Few adults pause to ask themselves why they feel anxious at the thought of checking a bank account balance, why they hesitate to invest despite having the means, or why they equate material possessions with self-worth. These behaviors are not random; they are echoes of early experiences. To deconstruct money scripts, one must first recognize that many current financial choices are not truly autonomous but are guided by the invisible hand of childhood conditioning.

Cultural Programming

Beyond the family unit, society itself plays a significant role in shaping financial identity. Cultural programming operates through media, education, and social norms, embedding collective beliefs about what wealth means and who deserves it. In many cultures, success is measured by outward displays of prosperity—cars, homes, vacations—rather than by financial stability or long-term security. This creates immense pressure to keep up appearances, even at the cost of debt and financial strain.

Advertising, in particular, has perfected the art of linking self-worth to consumption. A luxury watch is marketed not merely as a timekeeping device but as proof of success. A new car is positioned as a symbol of status. These messages, repeated endlessly, become internalized until spending to project an image feels natural, even necessary. In societies where individual achievement is celebrated above collective well-being, the belief takes root that wealth is a reflection of personal virtue, while financial struggle is interpreted as a sign of laziness or inadequacy. This narrative reinforces personal financial ceilings, as many internalize the idea that only certain types of people— those born into privilege, those who work themselves to exhaustion, or those who are extraordinarily lucky—deserve wealth.

The influence of cultural programming can be seen in how people respond to opportunities. Someone who grows up hearing that "money is the root of all evil" may unconsciously sabotage opportunities for financial growth, associating wealth with moral compromise. Another who absorbs the belief that "rich people are greedy" may hesitate to pursue financial abundance out of fear of becoming corrupt. Conversely, a culture that glorifies relentless accumulation without balance can produce individuals who equate self-worth with net worth, leaving them perpetually dissatisfied no matter how much they earn.

Recognizing cultural programming requires questioning the dominant narratives about money and success. Are we pursuing wealth to align with our values, or are we chasing symbols crafted by industries that profit from our insecurity? Deconstructing money scripts means unraveling these societal messages and deciding which ones we will consciously accept or reject.

Emotional Anchoring

If inherited beliefs and cultural programming provide the framework of money scripts, emotional anchoring cements them in place. Emotional anchoring occurs when past financial experiences leave strong imprints that dictate future behavior. These experiences may be moments of trauma, triumph, or loss, and they often generate recurring patterns of avoidance or obsession.

Consider someone who once invested in the stock market during a downturn and lost a significant portion of their savings. The pain of that experience can anchor them in fear, leading to a lifelong aversion to investing, even when opportunities are sound. Another person who grew up in poverty may experience such intense anxiety about reliving scarcity that they overwork, hoard, or become hyper-vigilant about financial security, sacrificing quality of life in the process. On the other hand, someone who once received a sudden windfall—perhaps a bonus or inheritance—may become anchored to the emotional high of abundance, leading them to chase risky ventures in hopes of recreating the euphoria.

The key to understanding emotional anchoring is recognizing that these responses are rarely about present reality. They are about the echo of past emotions projected onto current circumstances. Avoiding investments because of one past loss ignores the reality that markets are cyclical and that education can mitigate risk. Overworking to prevent imagined scarcity ignores the actual stability one may have already achieved. Chasing windfalls disregards the importance of steady, disciplined growth.

Healing from emotional anchoring requires disentangling current choices from past wounds. It involves acknowledging the emotions tied to earlier financial events and reframing them with new perspectives. For example, rather than seeing a financial loss as proof of incompetence, one can reinterpret it as a costly but valuable lesson that provides wisdom for future decisions. Emotional awareness allows individuals to act based on present goals rather than past pain.

Bringing It Together

Inherited beliefs, cultural programming, and emotional anchoring do not exist in isolation. Together, they form the psychological matrix that governs financial behavior. A person raised in a family that feared money, within a culture that glorifies consumption, and who has experienced financial trauma will face a vastly different financial reality than someone whose upbringing, culture, and experiences fostered trust, confidence, and resilience. These differences explain why the same financial advice produces dramatically different results for different people.

The Harvard study on lottery winners and self-made millionaires underscores this truth. Wealth given without the corresponding mindset quickly evaporates, while wealth rebuilt after loss is sustained because the mindset has already been forged. Understanding money scripts is the first step toward transforming one's financial life. By deconstructing the inherited beliefs, questioning cultural programming, and healing emotional anchors, individuals can begin to rewrite their scripts consciously, setting the stage for not just temporary success but lasting prosperity.

1.2 The Scarcity-to-Abundance Transition

At the core of financial transformation lies a shift in perspective that is as neurological as it is philosophical: the movement from a scarcity mindset to an abundance mindset. Scarcity thinking is rooted in survival. It is the mental framework that evolved in environments where resources were limited, and every decision was filtered through the lens of immediate safety and conservation. While useful in contexts of genuine threat, scarcity distorts judgment in modern financial life, where opportunities for growth and wealth creation often require delayed gratification, calculated risk, and vision beyond the immediate moment. Abundance thinking, by contrast, is not about reckless optimism or ignoring limitations but about recognizing that resources can expand, opportunities are ever-present, and one's choices play a significant role in shaping financial reality.

Neurologically, the brain under scarcity operates differently. Studies in behavioral economics and neuroscience show that when individuals feel deprived, cognitive bandwidth narrows. The prefrontal cortex—the area responsible for planning, reasoning, and long-term decision-making—becomes hijacked by the amygdala, which is primed for fight-or-flight responses. This is why people under financial stress may make decisions that seem irrational from the outside: payday loans, ignoring bills until they spiral, or declining investment opportunities for fear of loss. To shift toward abundance, practical rewiring is required, and this begins with practices that calm the survival centers of the brain while activating higher-order thinking.

One technique is mindfulness training, which interrupts the cycle of reactive financial behavior. By cultivating awareness of thoughts and emotions in the moment, individuals can pause before making scarcity-driven decisions. For example, rather than reacting to a sudden expense with panic and avoidance, a person trained in mindfulness can acknowledge the fear, detach from it, and then re-engage their rational faculties to evaluate options more clearly. Gratitude practices also play a critical role. When the mind is trained daily to focus on existing resources— health, relationships, skills, and even small financial wins—it begins to loosen the grip of scarcity and primes the brain for opportunity recognition. Neuroscience has shown that gratitude increases dopamine and serotonin activity, enhancing motivation and openness to growth.

Opportunity recognition is perhaps the most tangible benefit of the scarcity-to-abundance transition. When locked in scarcity, the mind becomes attuned to threats and blind to potential. A person who sees only the risk of losing money may ignore a chance to invest in education, start a side business, or acquire appreciating assets. By contrast, someone operating from abundance perceives options where others see dead ends. This shift does not happen overnight but develops with consistent retraining. Journaling about possibilities, surrounding oneself with examples of success, and engaging in environments where innovation and creativity are encouraged are all ways to reorient perception toward growth. What once looked like insurmountable barriers— such as starting a business with limited capital—become opportunities to innovate and leverage partnerships, technology, or unconventional funding sources.

Risk recalibration is another essential component of this transition. Scarcity creates an exaggerated perception of danger, leading either to paralysis or to reckless gambling. In both cases, the underlying mechanism is the same: distorted risk assessment. Someone with a scarcity mindset may hoard cash in a low-interest savings account for decades, fearful of investing, and thereby miss out on the compounding power of growth. Alternatively, in an attempt to break free from scarcity quickly, they may gamble on lottery tickets, speculative schemes, or high-risk investments without due diligence. Abundance thinking does not eliminate caution but refines it. It distinguishes between intelligent risk-taking—calculated, informed, and aligned with long-term goals—and reckless behavior driven by desperation.

Psychological frameworks for risk recalibration emphasize reframing risk as a spectrum rather than a binary choice of "safe" versus "dangerous." Intelligent risk is seen as an essential ingredient of wealth building, much like investing in higher education or pursuing entrepreneurial ventures. By studying probabilities, outcomes, and contingencies, individuals can learn to evaluate risk in a balanced way. This allows them to embrace opportunities that might once have seemed too intimidating while rejecting those that appeal only to quick-fix fantasies. Over time, this recalibration fosters resilience. When setbacks occur—and they inevitably will—the abundant thinker interprets them not as confirmation of doom but as feedback for refinement, whereas the scarcity-driven mind interprets them as proof that financial growth is impossible.

Thus, the transition from scarcity to abundance is not a matter of wishful thinking but of systematic rewiring. It involves calming the survival instincts of the brain, retraining perception to notice opportunities, and developing frameworks to assess risk intelligently. Once internalized, this shift opens the door to sustainable wealth creation, as it empowers individuals to act not from fear but from vision, not from desperation but from clarity.

1.3 Identity-Based Wealth Building

Once the scarcity-to-abundance transition is underway, the next stage in financial transformation is identity-based wealth building. At its core, this principle recognizes that sustainable financial success does not arise from isolated actions but from identity itself—the internalized self-concept that drives consistent behavior. Wealth is not simply something we achieve; it is something we become. To build and maintain wealth, one must adopt an identity aligned with abundance, discipline, and strategic growth.

The concept of the millionaire identity is not about copying the external trappings of wealthy individuals but about internalizing the thought patterns and decision-making processes that produce wealth. A person who identifies as someone capable of creating and sustaining prosperity naturally approaches decisions differently than someone who sees themselves as perpetually struggling. The millionaire identity prioritizes long-term rewards over immediate gratification, views challenges as stepping stones rather than obstacles, and treats financial setbacks as lessons rather than catastrophes. This identity is reinforced not by isolated choices but by a constellation of habits: consistent saving, deliberate investing, continuous learning, and disciplined spending.

The congruence principle lies at the heart of identity-based wealth building. It suggests that once an identity is firmly adopted, actions will naturally align with it, and any behavior that contradicts it will create internal tension. For example, if someone genuinely sees themselves as a disciplined wealth builder, splurging recklessly on status symbols will feel incongruent. Rather than requiring constant willpower, wealth-preserving behavior becomes a matter of self-consistency. The danger for many is that they hold onto identities that are inconsistent with wealth: identities of being "bad with money," of being "always broke," or of being someone who "just can't save." These self-concepts perpetuate self-sabotage because the unconscious mind works tirelessly to preserve internal consistency, even at the expense of external progress. Rewriting identity therefore becomes as critical as learning financial strategies.

Social environment design plays a decisive role in reinforcing or undermining this new identity. Human beings are profoundly shaped by their environments, often more than they realize. The adage that we become the average of the five people we spend the most time with is particularly true in financial life. If one's social circle normalizes debt, impulsive spending, and disdain for investing, it is difficult to sustain wealth-building habits, no matter how well-intentioned. By contrast, a community that values discipline, strategic growth, and open financial discussion strengthens the wealthy identity through reinforcement.

Designing a supportive environment involves more than choosing friends. It includes curating what one consumes in terms of media, books, podcasts, and online communities. Exposure to narratives of growth, innovation, and resilience builds a mental ecosystem that normalizes abundance and wealth-building behaviors. Even physical environment matters: a workspace designed for focus and clarity, a financial dashboard that makes progress visible, or a home environment that emphasizes intentional living all reinforce identity. When actions, surroundings, and relationships all align with the wealthy self-concept, progress becomes self-sustaining.

Identity-based wealth building is ultimately about transformation at the deepest level. Rather than relying on bursts of willpower, it aligns the subconscious mind with conscious goals, creating harmony between who we are and what we do. It shifts the question from "What financial strategies should I try?" to "Who must I become to achieve and sustain wealth?" When that identity is adopted and nurtured, the strategies become almost inevitable, because they are simply expressions of the self.

Together, the scarcity-to-abundance transition and identity-based wealth building form the twin pillars of the Wealth Mindset Matrix. One addresses the limitations of fear-driven thinking, and the other provides a new foundation rooted in aligned identity. When scarcity gives way to abundance and identity shifts from struggle to wealth, financial behavior ceases to be a battle against old habits and becomes a natural extension of who we are becoming.

Chapter 2: The Neuroscience of Financial Decision Making

Stanford neuroscientist Dr. Brian Knutson's research has shed light on a fascinating paradox of the human brain: the neural circuits responsible for reward often fire more intensely in anticipation of financial gain than in the actual moment of receiving it. This finding helps explain why so many people behave irrationally with money, chasing the thrill of possibility while neglecting the sober discipline required for lasting prosperity. Understanding the brain's role in financial behavior reveals that wealth is not simply a matter of external strategies or rational planning but of neural patterns that can either sabotage or support our goals. By exploring how dopamine, reward prediction errors, delayed gratification circuitry, and neuroplasticity shape decision-making, we begin to see why money triggers such powerful impulses and how these same mechanisms can be harnessed for more consistent, wealth-building choices.

2.1 The Dopamine-Driven Money Brain

At the heart of the brain's response to money is dopamine, a neurotransmitter often mischaracterized as the "pleasure chemical." In truth, dopamine is not about pleasure itself but about the motivation and anticipation that precede it. It drives us toward goals, heightens attention, and reinforces behaviors that promise reward. When it comes to financial decision-making, dopamine's role is double-edged. It can propel us toward productive effort and disciplined saving, but it can also lure us into addictive spending, compulsive gambling, or irrational investment bubbles.

One key mechanism in this process is the phenomenon of reward prediction errors. The brain constantly generates expectations about outcomes. When a reward exceeds expectations, dopamine surges, reinforcing the behavior that led to the surprise gain. Conversely, when outcomes fall short, dopamine levels dip, producing feelings of disappointment. This system, though adaptive in evolutionary terms, can create destructive cycles in modern financial life. A stock that suddenly jumps in value produces an outsized dopamine response, tempting investors to chase further gains even if fundamentals do not support it. A shopping spree that yields an unexpected bargain reinforces impulsive spending. Over time, the brain learns to crave the thrill of uncertainty itself, not the actual reward. This is why casinos thrive, why speculative bubbles form, and why consumers repeatedly buy items they neither need nor truly want.

The problem is compounded by the fact that the brain's reward circuitry adapts quickly. Once a particular gain becomes predictable, the dopamine response diminishes, driving individuals to seek new or greater risks to achieve the same neural "high." In the context of personal finance, this means that the joy of a first bonus or a successful investment can fade rapidly, leaving a void that people attempt to fill with riskier behaviors. This is one reason why sudden wealth, such as lottery winnings, often evaporates: without a recalibration of the brain's reward systems, the individual continues to chase anticipation, not stability.

Counterbalancing this dopamine-driven anticipation is the circuitry of delayed gratification, rooted in the prefrontal cortex. This part of the brain, particularly the dorsolateral prefrontal cortex, is responsible for executive functions such as planning, impulse control, and long-term strategy. When the prefrontal cortex is strong and engaged, individuals can resist the lure of immediate pleasure in favor of greater future rewards. This was famously demonstrated in the Stanford marshmallow experiment, where children who resisted eating a marshmallow immediately in order to receive two later demonstrated better life outcomes decades on. The principle applies directly to wealth building: the capacity to override the desire for instant gratification—to forgo impulsive spending in favor of saving, or to stay invested through market volatility rather than selling out of fear—is essential for long-term financial success.

The challenge is that the prefrontal cortex is energy-intensive and easily fatigued. Under stress, fatigue, or cognitive overload, its regulatory control weakens, allowing the dopamine-driven impulses of the limbic system to dominate. This explains why people often make poor financial decisions when they are tired, stressed, or emotionally overwhelmed. They reach for retail therapy after a hard day, panic-sell investments in the midst of economic uncertainty, or take out high-interest loans during periods of desperation. To strengthen the prefrontal cortex's role in financial decision-making, deliberate training is required. Practices such as meditation, cognitive behavioral techniques, and even structured financial planning exercises can enhance executive control, making it easier to delay gratification and stick to long-term strategies.

Perhaps the most encouraging aspect of neuroscience is the principle of neuroplasticity—the brain's capacity to reorganize itself by forming new neural connections throughout life. Financial behavior is not hardwired; it can be reshaped with intentional practice. Just as a pianist strengthens neural circuits related to finger dexterity through repetition, an individual can strengthen circuits related to disciplined financial decision-making through consistent exercises. For instance, the simple act of regularly automating savings rewires the brain to associate consistency with reward. Similarly, practicing visualization techniques—imagining the satisfaction of financial freedom, the security of a paid-off home, or the joy of funding a child's education—creates neural patterns that reinforce patience and strategic choices.

Repetition is crucial. Each time an individual resists the pull of an impulse purchase and instead channels funds toward an investment, the brain reinforces pathways associated with long-term gain. Over months and years, these pathways become default circuits, reducing the cognitive effort required to make disciplined choices. This is why small daily habits, such as tracking expenses or reviewing financial goals, carry disproportionate power: they are not just actions but neural training exercises that transform how the brain perceives and responds to money.

Importantly, neuroplasticity also provides a pathway to heal from destructive financial habits. Someone who has long associated money with anxiety or shame can, through deliberate reframing and practice, create new associations of confidence and empowerment. This requires confronting past experiences, identifying the emotions linked to financial decisions, and deliberately replacing them with new narratives and practices. Over time, the brain's wiring adapts, and what once triggered fear or avoidance can begin to trigger calm focus and opportunity recognition.

The dopamine-driven money brain explains why traditional financial advice so often falls flat. Simply telling someone to "save more" or "invest wisely" does not address the neural underpinnings that drive impulsive or fearful behavior. By understanding reward prediction errors, we see why people are drawn to financial gambles despite knowing the odds. By examining delayed gratification circuitry, we appreciate why even intelligent individuals struggle to act in their long-term interest when the lure of immediate pleasure is strong. By embracing neuroplasticity, we recognize that no one is doomed to repeat old patterns forever; the brain can be rewired, and financial behavior can be reshaped.

When these insights are applied, the implications are profound. A disciplined saver is not just someone with strong willpower but someone whose prefrontal cortex has been trained to consistently override impulses. A savvy investor is not simply rational but someone who has learned to navigate reward prediction errors, recognizing that anticipation is not the same as value. A person who transforms from financial chaos to stability has not just changed their external circumstances but has engaged in a deep neurological rewiring that makes new choices natural rather than forced.

The work of Dr. Knutson and other neuroscientists reveals that financial irrationality is not a moral failing but a predictable outcome of brain chemistry. More importantly, it shows that by bringing awareness to these mechanisms and engaging in intentional practice, individuals can align their brains with their financial goals. In doing so, they move beyond the cycles of impulse and regret into a steady, empowered relationship with money—one where anticipation no longer dictates action, and where wealth-building choices become not an uphill battle but a natural expression of a rewired mind.

2.2 Cognitive Biases in Wealth Building

One of the most striking insights from behavioral economics is that the human brain is not built to handle money rationally. Unlike food, shelter, or social connection, wealth is an abstract concept. Its value is symbolic, stored in digits, paper, or metal, and its future potential often outweighs its present reality. Because of this, financial decision-making is especially vulnerable to cognitive biases—systematic errors in thinking that distort judgment. These biases are not signs of weakness but natural consequences of how the brain evolved to handle uncertainty. To build lasting wealth, however, one must learn to recognize and neutralize them. Three of the most influential are loss aversion, confirmation bias, and anchoring.

Loss aversion is the tendency to feel the pain of losing something more intensely than the pleasure of gaining the same thing. Pioneering research by Daniel Kahneman and Amos Tversky demonstrated that people would rather avoid a loss of one hundred dollars than secure a gain of the same amount, even though the net effect is identical. This aversion often leads investors to cling to underperforming assets, unwilling to sell at a loss, or to avoid potentially profitable investments altogether for fear of losing money. The irony is that this defensive stance frequently leads to greater losses over time, as opportunities are missed and capital stagnates. Mastering loss aversion requires reframing the narrative around risk. Instead of viewing losses as personal failures, they must be seen as part of the inevitable variability of markets and as tuition in the school of wealth building. Historical data reveals that over long horizons, diversified investments tend to grow, even though short-term losses are unavoidable. By focusing attention on the trajectory rather than the temporary setback, individuals can gradually retrain their brains to tolerate volatility without panic.

Confirmation bias, another pervasive distortion, operates more subtly but can be equally destructive. It is the human tendency to seek out information that confirms preexisting beliefs while ignoring or discounting evidence that contradicts them. In financial life, this often manifests when investors latch onto news or data that supports their preferred strategy while disregarding warning signs. Someone convinced that a particular sector will boom may consume only optimistic analyses while dismissing critical reports, reinforcing an echo chamber that blinds them to risk. Neutralizing confirmation bias requires deliberate systems of disconfirmation. This might include actively seeking out contrarian perspectives, consulting advisors with different viewpoints, or setting rules that demand a structured devil's advocate approach before making large decisions. In essence, the discipline lies not in suppressing conviction but in ensuring that conviction is stress-tested by evidence. True confidence is forged not by avoiding contradiction but by wrestling with it until a more nuanced, resilient conclusion emerges.

Anchoring bias, meanwhile, operates by tethering financial judgments to arbitrary reference points. The first number the brain encounters in relation to a decision often exerts an outsized influence, regardless of its actual relevance. For instance, if a stock once traded at one hundred dollars per share, investors may treat that figure as its "true" value, even if changing fundamentals suggest otherwise. Similarly, individuals often anchor their sense of fair income or acceptable wealth to the salaries of their parents, their first job, or the averages in their social circle, thereby limiting what they believe is possible. Liberation from anchoring bias comes through cultivating flexibility. Rather than fixating on historical numbers or arbitrary comparisons, individuals must learn to ground their decisions in present evidence and future potential. This involves questioning whether the reference point is genuinely informative or simply convenient. Once freed from anchors, financial choices become more dynamic, responsive to reality rather than chained to outdated assumptions.

The cumulative effect of these biases is profound. Left unchecked, they create a feedback loop that traps individuals in mediocrity or decline. Fear of loss prevents bold action, selective attention blinds them to warning signs, and irrelevant anchors constrain ambition. Yet when these biases are understood and deliberately addressed, they become stepping stones rather than stumbling blocks. Awareness alone is not enough; it must be coupled with structured practices that consistently expose and challenge the distortions. Wealth building then becomes less about fighting markets and more about mastering the mind that navigates them.

2.3 Emotional Regulation for Financial Success

While cognitive biases distort judgment, emotions can completely derail it. Nowhere is this more evident than in moments of financial stress, when the amygdala—the brain's emotional command center—hijacks rational processing. Market volatility, sudden expenses, or economic downturns can trigger fight-or-flight responses, leading to impulsive decisions that sabotage long-term goals. Emotional regulation, therefore, is not a luxury but a necessity for financial success. The capacity to remain calm and clear-headed when money is at stake distinguishes those who build sustainable wealth from those who repeatedly undermine their own efforts.

Preventing amygdala hijacking begins with awareness of its onset. Signs include racing thoughts, heightened anxiety, and an urgent compulsion to act—sell, withdraw, spend, or escape. The problem is not the presence of emotion itself but the timing of action under its influence. Techniques such as deep breathing, grounding exercises, and short pauses before major financial decisions create space for the prefrontal cortex to reassert control. Some investors even implement "cooling-off periods," delaying trades or purchases for twenty-four hours to ensure that decisions are not purely reactive. Neurofeedback has also shown promise, training individuals to monitor and modulate their own neural activity, building resilience against emotional hijacking during financial turbulence.

Fear, in particular, is a powerful driver of poor financial choices. It often manifests as avoidance—failing to open bills, neglecting to review portfolios, or putting off essential conversations about money. Yet fear can also lead to rashness, such as panic-selling investments during a downturn or rushing into supposedly safe but unprofitable vehicles. Converting fear into motivated action requires cognitive restructuring, a psychological technique that reframes the meaning of financial challenges. Instead of interpreting volatility as catastrophe, one can reinterpret it as opportunity—a chance to acquire assets at lower prices or to reassess strategy with greater clarity. Fear ceases to paralyze when it is harnessed as fuel for learning and adaptation. Anxiety about money can become the spark for building new skills, diversifying income streams, or strengthening safety nets, rather than the excuse for retreat.

Confidence, however, must be calibrated with equal care. Excessive fear paralyzes, but excessive optimism blinds. Overconfidence can lead to over-leveraging, speculative gambles, or dismissing the need for professional advice. True financial mastery lies in balanced confidence—an equilibrium where optimism about the future is grounded in realistic appraisal of risks. Confidence calibration can be cultivated by maintaining feedback systems, such as tracking actual results against projections. When reality is consistently compared with expectation, both excessive pessimism and excessive optimism are tempered, producing a more stable mindset. This balance prevents the twin traps of timidity and recklessness, allowing individuals to act with courage without veering into hubris.

Emotional regulation is ultimately about maintaining alignment between long-term goals and short-term reactions. Wealth is built not in moments of triumph but in the quiet discipline of consistent choices, made steadily even when markets tremble or fear whispers. To regulate emotions is to preserve clarity in the midst of noise, to respond deliberately rather than reactively. It transforms the financial journey from a rollercoaster of highs and lows into a purposeful climb toward stability and abundance.

The intersection of cognitive biases and emotional regulation is where neuroscience and psychology meet practical finance. Biases warp perception, while emotions hijack control. But both can be trained, managed, and even transformed into strengths. A disciplined investor or entrepreneur is not someone devoid of fear or bias but someone who recognizes them, creates systems to counteract them, and consistently returns to alignment with long-term vision. This mastery of mind is what turns financial strategies into enduring wealth, bridging the gap between knowledge and execution.

Chapter 3: The Psychology of Income Expansion

A groundbreaking study from Yale University revealed that individuals who negotiated their very first job offer went on to earn, on average, half a million dollars more across their careers than those who accepted what was initially placed on the table. The significance of this finding is not only financial but deeply psychological. It illustrates that income is rarely a simple function of skill or market demand; it is profoundly shaped by mindset, belief systems, and the capacity to advocate for one's worth. Those who never question the value assigned to them often plateau early, while those who challenge assumptions, negotiate, and expand their comfort zones consistently break through invisible ceilings. To truly grow income, one must address not only external opportunities but also the internal barriers that quietly dictate what we believe we deserve.

3.1 Breaking Income Ceilings

Income ceilings are not merely imposed by employers, industries, or economies. More often than not, they are self-imposed, built from layers of unconscious beliefs that create psychological comfort zones around earning potential. These ceilings act like thermostats: when income rises above a certain level, self-sabotage often pulls it back down, just as when it falls too low, survival instincts may push it back up. The mind, conditioned by years of inherited scripts, cultural influences, and personal experiences, becomes calibrated to a "normal" range of income that feels safe, even if that range is far below one's true potential. Breaking these ceilings requires uncovering and dismantling the invisible narratives that govern what we believe we can earn, followed by deliberate cultivation of new skills that align inner worth with external reward.

The first of these barriers is the psychological salary limit. Many people carry unexamined beliefs about what constitutes "enough." These beliefs often stem from childhood observations. A person who grew up in a household where the annual income never exceeded a modest sum may unconsciously adopt that figure as a reference point for their own career, even in completely different industries. Without realizing it, they reject opportunities that would catapult them beyond that limit, rationalizing their decisions with excuses such as "I'm not ready," "That's unrealistic," or "I don't want to be greedy." These internal scripts prevent them from even pursuing roles or business ventures that could yield far greater income. To dismantle these barriers, one must first bring them into awareness, asking questions such as: What do I believe is the maximum I can earn in a year? Where did that belief originate? Does it reflect objective reality or inherited limitation? This introspection exposes the arbitrary nature of most income ceilings and opens the door to redefining them.

Once psychological barriers are identified, the next step is cultivating value recognition. Many individuals chronically underestimate their own worth, not because their skills lack value but because they have never been trained to recognize and articulate it. Employers and clients rarely compensate based on intrinsic worth alone; they respond to the ability to present and defend that worth convincingly. Value recognition begins with a shift in perspective: moving from an internal monologue of doubt to a clear-eyed appraisal of how one's skills, experiences, and efforts create tangible results for others. This requires documenting achievements, measuring impact, and learning to express them in terms that resonate with decision-makers. For example, instead of vaguely claiming to be a "hard worker," one might demonstrate how a project they led increased efficiency by twenty percent, saving the company thousands of dollars. By framing contributions in measurable outcomes, individuals not only recognize their own value but train others to see it as undeniable.

The failure to recognize and express value often intertwines with imposter syndrome, a psychological pattern where competent and capable people doubt their abilities and fear being exposed as frauds. Imposter syndrome can be particularly destructive in financial contexts, as it leads individuals to undersell themselves, avoid asking for raises, or decline opportunities they feel unworthy of. The irony is that those most afflicted are often the most competent, because their awareness of what they don't know magnifies their insecurities. Breaking free from imposter syndrome is not about silencing self-doubt entirely but about transforming it into a catalyst for growth. When reframed, the sense of inadequacy can fuel continuous learning and skill development, ensuring that competence expands alongside confidence. The key lies in shifting the internal narrative from "I don't belong here" to "I am capable of learning whatever is required to excel here." In this way, imposter feelings become an engine of strategic development rather than a brake on ambition.

Transforming income ceilings also requires practicing negotiation as both a skill and a mindset. The Yale study underscores that the act of negotiating is itself a signal—to oneself as much as to others—that one's value is not fixed but dynamic. Negotiation requires confronting discomfort, risking rejection, and asserting worth in the face of potential disapproval. For those conditioned by scarcity or deference, this can feel unnatural, even threatening. Yet every negotiation, successful or not, stretches the boundaries of perceived income potential. Even when an employer refuses, the act of asking reprograms the mind to expect more, breaking the psychological ceiling that once confined it.

The consequences of breaking income ceilings extend beyond salary. They ripple into entrepreneurship, investment, and creative pursuits. An entrepreneur who clings to the belief that clients will never pay beyond a certain price point will sabotage their business by underpricing and overworking. An investor who cannot imagine themselves holding substantial wealth may unconsciously liquidate positions too early, robbing themselves of compounding returns. In each case, the internal ceiling becomes the invisible hand guiding decisions. Conversely, when ceilings are lifted, individuals begin to notice opportunities previously hidden. They see the possibility of scaling a business, leveraging partnerships, or positioning themselves for leadership roles that once seemed unattainable.

The journey to break income ceilings is therefore both psychological and practical. It begins with identifying the inherited and internalized limits that define what feels normal. It continues with training the mind to recognize and assert value, transforming self-doubt into a driver of competence, and practicing the art of negotiation. As each barrier falls, the ceiling rises, and with it, the capacity to align income with true potential.

Over time, this process creates not just higher earnings but a fundamentally new relationship with money—one no longer defined by unconscious limitations but by conscious expansion.

Income expansion, then, is not a matter of luck or external circumstance alone. It is a function of psychology, self-perception, and the courage to challenge invisible boundaries. Just as the Yale study revealed, the difference between those who accept what they are given and those who negotiate is not merely in the immediate outcome but in the trajectory of their lives. Those who break ceilings once learn to break them again, until the very concept of limitation dissolves. At that point, income ceases to be constrained by old beliefs and begins to reflect the limitless potential of a mind that has been freed.

3.2 The Strategic Career Acceleration Model

The expansion of income is rarely the result of a single decision or isolated skill. More often, it emerges from a deliberate strategy that compounds value over time by combining abilities, networks, and authority in ways that set an individual apart. This approach, which can be described as the Strategic Career Acceleration Model, emphasizes not just working harder but positioning oneself so that opportunities naturally gravitate toward one's unique blend of capabilities. At its core are three psychological levers: stacking skills, maximizing the power of networks, and cultivating authority in a chosen domain.

Skill stacking represents a profound shift in how one thinks about expertise. The traditional model of career development prizes specialization—becoming the best in a narrow field. While mastery in a single area remains important, modern markets often reward those who can integrate multiple competencies into distinctive combinations. The psychology of skill stacking lies in understanding that the brain adapts most efficiently when new learning builds upon existing knowledge, creating a compound effect. A financial analyst who adds persuasive communication skills becomes more effective in leadership roles. A software engineer who learns design thinking can bridge the gap between technical development and user experience. Each additional layer of skill interacts with the others, creating intersections where few competitors operate. The result is not just incremental improvement but exponential differentiation, as one's professional identity becomes increasingly difficult to replicate.

Maximizing the network effect requires an equally intentional psychological orientation. Many people view networking as transactional—collecting contacts or attending events in the hope of immediate benefit. Yet the true power of relationships lies in how the human mind responds to trust, reciprocity, and social proof. Opportunities often arise not directly from those we know but from the extended networks they open. Psychologically, this is driven by the principle of social contagion, where behaviors, attitudes, and opportunities spread through interconnected webs of relationships. The person who invests in authentic connections, offering value without immediate expectation of return, primes their network to reciprocate in unpredictable yet powerful ways. Over time, the probability of serendipitous introductions, referrals, and collaborations multiplies, accelerating career growth in ways no single effort could achieve. This is not simply about knowing more people but about cultivating genuine influence within networks so that one's name naturally surfaces when opportunities arise.

Authority building completes the model by solidifying perception. In an age saturated with information, the human brain gravitates toward perceived leaders as a way of simplifying decision-making. Authority is not an accident but the outcome of consistently demonstrating expertise and insight in visible ways. This requires both the mindset to view one's knowledge as valuable to others and the discipline to share it strategically. Writing articles, producing content, speaking publicly, or teaching are not mere add-ons to a career—they are psychological signals that elevate credibility. Each act of thought leadership conditions both the self and the market to perceive greater value. The individual begins to see themselves as an authority, which fuels confidence, while others begin to associate their name with trust and competence. This dynamic, once established, creates a feedback loop where opportunities compound.

Together, skill stacking, network maximization, and authority building form a framework for career acceleration that transcends linear growth. Rather than climbing a predictable ladder step by step, individuals who apply this model create inflection points— moments where the accumulation of layered skills, expanded networks, and recognized authority catapult them forward. The acceleration is not random but the result of psychological strategies applied deliberately over time. By seeing career growth as an interplay of internal development and external positioning, one can consistently expand income in ways that appear effortless to outside observers but are in fact the product of strategic design.

3.3 Entrepreneurial Psychology Mastery

While career acceleration within established structures can significantly expand income, the psychology of entrepreneurship offers a different but equally powerful path. Unlike salaried roles, entrepreneurship places the individual directly in the realm of creation, where risks and rewards are amplified. Success depends less on technical knowledge and more on the ability to navigate uncertainty, sustain vision through obstacles, and expand one's thinking to match the scale of emerging opportunities. Entrepreneurial psychology, therefore, is not about suppressing fear or blind optimism but about calibrating mindset to thrive in the volatile landscape of business.

Risk tolerance is the first dimension of this mastery. Human beings are naturally loss-averse, and for many, the idea of leaving a stable paycheck for uncertain returns feels insurmountable. Yet entrepreneurship requires comfort with ambiguity, as no venture begins with guarantees. The psychological challenge is not to eliminate fear but to calibrate it. Those with too little risk tolerance hesitate endlessly, missing opportunities, while those with too much dive recklessly into ventures without preparation. The optimal mindset treats risk as a spectrum, where uncertainty is analyzed, mitigated, and balanced with potential reward. This requires reframing setbacks not as catastrophic losses but as experiments that yield valuable data. Entrepreneurs who thrive see each failure as an iteration rather than an endpoint, allowing them to remain engaged despite volatility. Over time, this reframing builds resilience, making the unknown less paralyzing and more navigable.

Vision-to-reality translation represents the second dimension. Starting a business often begins with an idea that inspires enthusiasm, but enthusiasm alone cannot carry one through the inevitable challenges. The psychology of translation involves sustaining motivation when the glow of the original vision fades in the face of obstacles. This demands mental models that anchor attention on process rather than outcome. Breaking goals into incremental milestones creates a sense of progress, activating the brain's reward system and sustaining engagement. Visualization techniques also play a role, as imagining the future state in vivid detail primes the brain to act in alignment with that reality. Yet the most powerful driver is purpose—connecting the entrepreneurial vision to deeper values beyond profit. When setbacks occur, a purpose-rooted entrepreneur interprets them as obstacles on the path rather than as invalidations of the journey. This capacity to carry vision forward despite turbulence is one of the clearest psychological markers of entrepreneurial success.

The third dimension, scale-thinking development, elevates entrepreneurship from survival to legacy. Many entrepreneurs remain trapped in small-scale operations, not because markets limit them but because their mental frameworks do. Scale-thinking requires expanding one's cognitive map to conceive of opportunities on a much larger canvas. It involves asking not just how to serve a handful of customers but how to design systems, partnerships, and innovations that can serve thousands or millions. Psychologically, this expansion demands a shift from an individual contributor identity to that of a systems builder. It requires letting go of control, delegating effectively, and trusting others to carry the vision forward. Scale-thinking also involves tolerance for complexity, as larger opportunities inevitably introduce layers of challenge. Those who expand their capacity to manage ambiguity, adapt structures, and maintain clarity of vision in the midst of growing demands unlock income levels unattainable in smaller frames of reference.

Entrepreneurial psychology mastery, then, is not about luck or charisma but about mental orientation. It combines calibrated risk tolerance, resilient vision, and expansive thinking into a framework that sustains ventures through uncertainty and positions them for exponential growth. Entrepreneurs who embody this mastery transform not only their own financial trajectories but also the ecosystems around them, creating opportunities for others and multiplying impact.

When paired with the Strategic Career Acceleration Model, entrepreneurial psychology highlights that income expansion is not confined to either employment or entrepreneurship but to the mindset applied in either path. Whether within an organization or in building one, the psychological levers of growth remain the same: dismantling internal barriers, amplifying value, building networks of opportunity, and maintaining resilience in the face of volatility. It is this inner mastery that ultimately determines how high income can rise and how sustainable wealth can become.

Chapter 4: Investment Psychology and Market Behavior

Warren Buffett's enduring wisdom—"Be fearful when others are greedy and greedy when others are fearful"—remains one of the clearest distillations of the psychological edge required in investing. Markets do not move solely because of fundamentals; they rise and fall based on human behavior. Fear and euphoria ripple through crowds of investors, shaping prices as much as balance sheets or quarterly reports. The ability to detach from the herd and act with clarity when others are swept away by emotion is not simply a matter of strategy but of psychology. Master investors distinguish themselves not by having access to secret information but by cultivating mental frameworks that allow them to resist collective impulses.

4.1 Contrarian Thinking Development

Contrarian thinking is not about reflexively opposing the majority for the sake of being different. It is about developing the psychological discipline to maintain independent analysis, even when the crowd pressures conformity. The human brain is wired for herd behavior. In evolutionary terms, survival depended on belonging to the group, reading signals of danger from others, and aligning behavior with the collective. In financial markets, however, this wiring becomes a liability. During bubbles, when optimism inflates valuations beyond reason, the herd creates a seductive illusion of safety in numbers. During panics, when fear drives indiscriminate selling, the same herd instills terror that blinds investors to opportunity. To cultivate contrarian thinking, one must train the mind to observe these cycles without becoming trapped in them.

Resisting herd mentality begins with an awareness of how social proof operates. The brain takes shortcuts when faced with uncertainty, and one of the most powerful shortcuts is assuming that if many people are doing something, it must be correct. This is why investors pile into hot stocks at peaks or flee markets at bottoms, despite evidence that such behavior undermines long-term returns. The antidote lies in building confidence in independent frameworks of analysis. This does not mean ignoring consensus entirely, but rather developing criteria for decisions that are rooted in evidence rather than emotion. For example, an investor committed to value-based principles may watch as prices soar during speculative manias but refrain from joining simply because "everyone else is making money." The discipline to endure feelings of missing out is central to resisting the pull of the herd. Similarly, in downturns, when others are paralyzed by fear, the contrarian mind looks for assets that remain fundamentally strong but temporarily undervalued.

One of the greatest accelerants of herd behavior in modern markets is the media. Financial news cycles thrive on immediacy and emotion because these generate attention and engagement. Headlines scream of crashes, bubbles, or unprecedented opportunities, amplifying the psychological intensity investors already feel. Yet the media's incentives are rarely aligned with individual wealth building. Their goal is not to provide calm, measured analysis but to capture eyes and clicks. Developing immunity to media influence requires constructing mental filters. This means distinguishing between information that is genuinely useful—such as company earnings reports, regulatory changes, or macroeconomic data—and information designed to provoke emotion. Investors who cultivate these filters learn to treat media as background noise rather than decision-making guidance.

Training oneself to recognize emotional language in financial commentary is one practical approach. Words like "panic," "soar," "collapse," or "frenzy" are red flags that signal emotional framing rather than objective reporting. Another is limiting exposure during volatile periods. Just as a dieter avoids environments filled with temptation, disciplined investors may choose to step back from constant newsfeeds during market turmoil, relying instead on pre-established frameworks and long-term strategy. By controlling attention, one controls emotional reactivity, ensuring that decisions are guided by analysis rather than manipulated sentiment.

Contrarian confidence building completes the development of independent thinking. It is not enough to identify when the crowd is wrong; one must also have the conviction to act against it. This conviction is not arrogance but a disciplined trust in one's process. Confidence arises from preparation: studying historical cycles, back-testing strategies, and internalizing the knowledge that markets have always oscillated between fear and greed. The investor who understands that today's panic mirrors dozens of similar panics in the past develops the courage to step in when others flee. Similarly, the one who knows that bubbles inevitably burst has the fortitude to exit positions while euphoria still reigns.

Conviction, however, is strengthened not by blind stubbornness but by evidence-based practice. A contrarian investor learns to document their reasoning, evaluate assumptions, and track outcomes over time. This not only sharpens decision-making but creates a feedback loop of confidence: when past contrarian actions, grounded in solid analysis, lead to favorable results, the mind gradually accepts that resisting the crowd is not reckless but prudent. Confidence also grows through incremental exposure. Just as muscles strengthen under repeated stress, psychological resilience grows each time one endures the discomfort of standing apart from the herd and witnesses the benefits in hindsight.

The difficulty of contrarian thinking is that it requires embracing short-term discomfort for long-term advantage. In the moment, resisting the herd can feel isolating and even foolish. Friends and colleagues may question decisions, media may amplify the opposite narrative, and the immediate market direction may punish contrarians before rewarding them. This is why contrarian psychology requires both patience and resilience. The reward is that, over time, contrarians capture opportunities others overlook, buying when assets are undervalued and avoiding losses when euphoria blinds the majority.

Ultimately, contrarian thinking development is not about being contrarian for its own sake. It is about aligning with truth over trend, analysis over emotion, and independence over conformity. Buffett's maxim reflects not a rule of thumb but a psychological orientation: to see fear and greed not as signals to follow but as indicators of when to pause, reflect, and often move in the opposite direction. By resisting herd mentality, filtering media noise, and cultivating conviction, the investor builds a mental edge that transcends technical skill. Markets will always swing between extremes, but those who master their own psychology position themselves not only to endure the cycles but to prosper because of them.

4.2 Long-Term Thinking Psychology

The most powerful force in investing is not a clever strategy or a rare insight but the passage of time combined with patience. Albert Einstein famously referred to compound interest as the eighth wonder of the world, yet for many investors, its power remains more theoretical than real. The human brain struggles with exponential growth because it evolved in environments where linear progress—walking a mile, hunting for food—dominated daily life. Our psychology is geared to expect incremental outcomes, not the astonishing acceleration that occurs when returns compound year after year. To adopt a long-term mindset, investors must deliberately train themselves to visualize and internalize how compounding works.

Compound interest visualization is best understood by imagining not the addition of money but the multiplication of possibilities. The brain more easily grasps stories and images than abstract numbers, which is why simple parables often make the concept vivid. Consider a single penny doubled each day for thirty days. While the early days appear insignificant—just a few cents, then a few dollars—by the thirtieth day the result exceeds five million dollars. The leap defies intuition, and that is the very point: wealth grows invisibly in its early stages and explosively in its later stages, provided discipline is maintained. Investors who internalize this truth are less likely to be discouraged by slow beginnings or tempted to disrupt compounding by chasing quick wins. Visualization techniques, such as projecting one's savings on a graph that extends decades into the future, allow the brain to see exponential curves rather than flat lines, embedding patience as a psychological reflex.

The temptation to abandon long-term strategies often arises from the allure of market timing. The mind is attracted to the idea that if one can predict the peaks and troughs of markets, wealth can be accumulated faster with less risk. Yet study after study demonstrates that consistent market timing is nearly impossible, even for professionals. The psychological danger is that successful timing once or twice creates overconfidence, leading to repeated attempts until mistakes outweigh earlier luck. The fallacy lies in confusing randomness with skill. Investors anchored to the belief that they can forecast short-term swings often end up eroding returns through excessive trading, higher costs, and missed opportunities when markets turn unexpectedly.

The antidote to the market timing fallacy is cultivating humility about uncertainty. Psychological frameworks that emphasize probability rather than prediction help counteract the illusion of control. Instead of asking, "Where will the market go next week?" the disciplined investor asks, "What range of outcomes is plausible, and how can my portfolio be resilient to them?" This shift reduces the emotional rollercoaster of constantly reacting to short-term noise. Accepting that volatility is not a signal to act but a natural feature of markets allows the long-term thinker to remain steady, focusing on the horizon rather than the turbulence of the present.

Diversification psychology plays a crucial role in sustaining this steadiness. While diversification is universally recommended, many investors fail to implement it effectively because cognitive biases distort judgment. Familiarity bias leads people to over-concentrate in assets they know, such as domestic stocks or companies in industries they work in. Overconfidence bias tempts them to believe their insights about a single stock or sector will outperform, leading to risky concentration. Recency bias convinces them that whatever has done well recently will continue to do so indefinitely, resulting in portfolios overloaded with yesterday's winners. Each of these biases narrows the range of holdings, undermining the protective effect of diversification.

To counteract these distortions, diversification must be approached not merely as a strategy but as a system. This means adopting allocation frameworks that are decided in advance and adhered to regardless of emotions or market narratives. By treating diversification as an expression of humility—the acknowledgment that no one can perfectly predict the future—investors align their psychology with reality. Diversification becomes not a reluctant compromise but a confident choice to accept uncertainty and manage it wisely. When properly understood, it is the psychological foundation of long-term thinking, creating the stability necessary to let compounding work unhindered.

4.3 Behavioral Portfolio Management

Even with long-term principles in place, the greatest threat to sustained wealth accumulation often comes not from markets but from the investor's own behavior. Behavioral portfolio management recognizes that humans are emotional beings, prone to overreaction, impatience, and distorted expectations. To succeed, portfolios must be managed not only in financial terms but also in psychological ones, providing structures that protect against destructive impulses.

One of the most common pitfalls is emotional volatility during downturns. When markets fall sharply, fear triggers survival instincts. The amygdala floods the brain with stress signals, urging immediate action to escape perceived danger. The result is panic selling, locking in losses that might have been temporary. Emotional volatility buffers are psychological safety nets designed to prevent such reactions. These buffers can take many forms: maintaining an emergency cash reserve to reduce the sense of vulnerability, predetermining thresholds for rebalancing instead of selling, or simply framing downturns as opportunities to acquire assets at discounted prices. By building emotional cushions, investors create the psychological distance necessary to ride through storms without abandoning their long-term plan.

Systematic decision-making further strengthens resilience by reducing reliance on willpower in moments of stress. Predefined criteria, such as asset allocation targets, automatic contributions, or rebalancing rules, transform investing from an emotional battlefield into a disciplined routine. Automation is particularly powerful because it bypasses the temptation to constantly intervene. By setting systems that operate independently of mood or fear, investors protect themselves from their own impulses. The brain, freed from the constant burden of deciding whether to act, learns to trust the process. This trust reduces anxiety and builds consistency, allowing compounding to function without interruption.

Performance attribution psychology adds another crucial dimension. Investors often misinterpret their results, attributing success to skill when it may be due to luck, or blaming themselves harshly for outcomes driven by factors beyond their control. Overconfidence born of temporary success can lead to reckless risk-taking, while repeated disappointments can foster learned helplessness, where individuals believe their actions have no effect and withdraw from active wealth building altogether. Both extremes are destructive, and both stem from distorted attribution.

To maintain balance, investors must cultivate accurate performance narratives. This means consistently reviewing not just outcomes but the quality of decisions. A good decision can sometimes lead to a poor outcome due to randomness, just as a bad decision can occasionally be rewarded. By focusing on the decision-making process rather than only the result, investors develop realistic expectations and avoid overreacting to short-term swings. This mindset mirrors the discipline of professional gamblers or scientists, who recognize that variance is inevitable but skill emerges over the long run.

Behavioral portfolio management is ultimately about designing an environment where the natural flaws of human psychology are acknowledged and mitigated rather than ignored. By creating buffers against emotional volatility, relying on systematic processes, and interpreting performance accurately, investors build resilience. They no longer depend solely on self-control in moments of crisis but rely on structures that guide them safely through turbulence.

When combined with the principles of long-term thinking, behavioral portfolio management forms the backbone of sustainable wealth creation. It acknowledges that while markets are unpredictable, human behavior is predictably vulnerable. The investor who prepares for their own psychological tendencies gains an advantage over those who believe they can simply outthink or outmuscle their emotions. True mastery in investing lies not in eliminating fear or greed but in constructing frameworks that prevent these emotions from dictating action.

In this way, psychology becomes not the enemy of investing but its greatest ally. By embracing the limits of the mind and designing strategies that protect against them, investors unlock the ability to endure volatility, harness compounding, and steadily build wealth across decades. The result is not just financial growth but a profound sense of stability, rooted in the knowledge that one's portfolio is not at the mercy of impulse but guided by discipline, patience, and resilience.

Chapter 5: The Wealth Attraction Paradox

Psychological research has repeatedly demonstrated that the highest earners and most fulfilled professionals are rarely those who chase money for its own sake. Instead, the evidence reveals a counterintuitive truth: people intrinsically motivated by autonomy, mastery, and purpose consistently outperform those whose primary driver is financial reward. One study showed that individuals led by deeper internal motivators earned roughly thirty percent more over their lifetimes than their money-driven peers. This paradox—wealth flowing most abundantly to those who do not focus on it directly—challenges many traditional notions of success. It suggests that prosperity is not the product of relentless pursuit but the natural byproduct of creating authentic value.

5.1 Indirect Wealth Creation Strategies

The paradox of wealth attraction can be understood through the psychology of value-first thinking. In markets, wealth flows to those who solve problems, ease pain points, or deliver joy and transformation. Yet the human tendency to fixate on personal gain often blinds people to the real source of income: the degree to which they serve others. Value-first psychology reframes the question from "How can I make money?" to "What problems can I solve, and for whom?" This subtle shift unleashes a different kind of creativity and motivation. When one is absorbed in service, money ceases to be the central goal yet arrives as an inevitable consequence of creating meaningful impact.

This principle can be seen in countless stories of entrepreneurs and professionals who achieved extraordinary success not by obsessing over income but by focusing intently on improving lives. A teacher who refines innovative methods to help struggling students eventually finds opportunities to publish materials, give talks, or develop online platforms. A designer who becomes fixated on solving accessibility challenges ends up creating products with wide market demand. Their financial outcomes are indirect—arriving not because they demanded wealth but because they prioritized service and allowed wealth to follow. The psychological mechanism is powerful: when the mind shifts from scarcity-driven self-interest to abundant service orientation, it naturally sees opportunities others miss. This is because the brain no longer evaluates every situation with the narrow lens of "what's in it for me" but instead perceives broader possibilities for creating value.

Passion-profit alignment deepens this effect by integrating personal authenticity with market need. Many people mistakenly believe that monetizing passion means abandoning practicality. Yet the psychology of sustainable income suggests otherwise. When individuals work from authentic interest, they access reservoirs of energy and persistence unavailable in pursuits driven only by external reward. Passion sustains effort when results are slow, when obstacles arise, and when motivation wanes. The key lies in aligning passion with market reality. A person fascinated by music may not thrive financially as a performer in a saturated market, but their passion could translate into teaching, producing, or developing innovative tools for learners. The alignment requires honest self-reflection: identifying what truly excites one at a deep level, and then mapping that excitement onto real problems people are willing to pay to solve.

Psychological techniques can support this process of alignment. Journaling about peak experiences, reflecting on times when work felt effortless, or experimenting with side projects can reveal passions hidden beneath the routines of daily life. Once identified, these passions must be tested against external feedback. Passion alone does not guarantee profit, but passion coupled with adaptability creates powerful opportunities. By iterating between what excites internally and what resonates externally, individuals can find niches where work feels meaningful and income flows steadily. When passion and profit converge, wealth no longer feels like a chase but a natural extension of living authentically.

Perhaps the most profound dimension of indirect wealth creation lies in what psychologists call flow—the optimal state of human performance described by Mihaly Csikszentmihalyi. Flow arises when challenge meets skill in perfect balance, drawing individuals into complete absorption where time seems to vanish and performance peaks. In this state, the brain releases dopamine, norepinephrine, and endorphins, enhancing focus, creativity, and efficiency. The economics of flow are powerful: individuals who regularly access this state produce work of such quality and intensity that it commands premium compensation. Athletes in flow break records, artists in flow create masterpieces, and entrepreneurs in flow innovate solutions that disrupt industries.

The path to leveraging flow in wealth creation begins with identifying activities that naturally induce it. These are often the tasks where one feels energized rather than drained, where hours pass unnoticed, and where effort feels intrinsically rewarding. By structuring work around these activities, individuals not only experience greater fulfillment but also produce outputs that are rare and valuable. For example, a software developer who finds flow in solving complex coding challenges may create tools that revolutionize efficiency for entire companies. Because flow amplifies productivity exponentially, those who harness it contribute disproportionately more value than peers, and markets reward them accordingly.

However, accessing flow consistently requires deliberate design. Environments free of constant distraction, goals that stretch but do not overwhelm, and feedback loops that confirm progress all increase the likelihood of entering flow states. By cultivating these conditions, individuals transform work from a grind into a channel of heightened creativity and achievement. Over time, the economic rewards compound because flow-driven outputs tend to stand apart in quality, innovation, and impact. The paradox deepens here: the more one becomes absorbed in the joy of work itself, the less one fixates on money, yet the more money arrives as a reflection of that exceptional contribution.

Indirect wealth creation strategies ultimately rest on the recognition that money is a trailing indicator, not a leading one. It follows value, passion, and performance rather than preceding them. Those who place money as the primary target often grow disillusioned, chasing outcomes without cultivating the underlying conditions that produce them. Those who shift focus to service, alignment, and flow, however, find that income expands naturally, often beyond what they imagined possible. This is the paradox: wealth is attracted, not pursued.

Seen through this lens, financial prosperity is less about tactical maneuvers and more about psychological orientation. It is about trusting that markets reward consistent value, that authentic passion fuels resilience, and that flow transforms effort into brilliance. The individuals who embrace these principles embody a subtle confidence, knowing that their focus on creating rather than chasing will draw opportunities, relationships, and compensation. They are not naïve about the role of money but understand that by putting it in its proper place—as an outcome rather than the objective—they position themselves for both fulfillment and abundance.

The wealth attraction paradox does not reject financial ambition but reframes it. It suggests that instead of demanding wealth directly, we cultivate the qualities that make wealth inevitable. By practicing value-first psychology, aligning passion with profitable application, and deliberately seeking flow states, individuals create an upward spiral where meaning and money reinforce each other. The path may appear indirect, but it is far more sustainable and rewarding than the relentless pursuit of money for its own sake. Over time, this approach not only expands income but transforms one's relationship with work, success, and life itself.

5.2 Abundance Thinking Applications

Abundance thinking is the natural extension of the wealth attraction paradox. Whereas scarcity thinking views the world as a fixed pie in which one person's gain must be another's loss, abundance recognizes that wealth can be created, expanded, and shared in ways that elevate all participants. This shift from zero-sum to collaborative opportunity is not merely philosophical; it has profound psychological and financial implications. Those who adopt abundance thinking consistently create richer networks, more resilient partnerships, and opportunities that scarcity thinkers never perceive.

Collaborative wealth building begins with this rejection of zero-sum assumptions. In business, careers, and investments, scarcity often breeds defensive competition: guarding information, hoarding opportunities, and treating others as rivals to be outmaneuvered. Yet history shows that some of the greatest fortunes have been built not in isolation but through partnerships where the combined talents of individuals produced outcomes far beyond what either could achieve alone. The psychology of collaboration works because human beings are wired for reciprocity. When one creates opportunities for others, others in turn seek ways to reciprocate, fueling a cycle of shared success. In practical terms, this might look like joint ventures, co-authorship, cross-promotion, or investment syndicates. What matters most is the mindset: shifting from "How can I maximize only my gain?" to "How can we expand the pie together?" The paradox is that by creating win-win arrangements, one often achieves greater wealth individually than by hoarding opportunities.

Generosity psychology deepens this truth. While conventional logic might suggest that giving reduces resources, research on prosocial behavior demonstrates the opposite. Strategic generosity creates goodwill, strengthens networks, and increases influence in ways that compound financially over time. When individuals give—whether through mentoring, sharing resources, or even financial contributions—they activate powerful psychological dynamics in others: gratitude, loyalty, and trust. These intangibles translate into tangible returns as doors open, referrals flow, and reputations grow. The concept of "karma economics" captures this dynamic. By creating value for others without immediate expectation, one seeds the ground for opportunities that may bloom unpredictably yet abundantly. Generosity, when genuine, creates a reputation that money cannot buy but that inevitably attracts more money. The wealthiest individuals throughout history, from industrial magnates to modern entrepreneurs, have often been noted for their philanthropy, not only as an outcome of wealth but as a reinforcing mechanism that secured their influence and legacy.

Gratitude-based attraction complements collaboration and generosity by shaping the inner state from which opportunities are perceived and acted upon. Gratitude is more than a polite social habit; it is a psychological practice that rewires the brain to notice abundance rather than lack. Neuroscience shows that gratitude enhances dopamine and serotonin pathways, both of which improve mood, motivation, and creativity. An individual steeped in gratitude approaches challenges not with despair but with curiosity and resilience, making them more likely to persist until opportunities emerge. On a social level, grateful individuals radiate positivity, drawing others toward them and creating networks rich with trust and goodwill. In financial life, this magnetism translates into opportunities for deals, partnerships, and unexpected offers. By cultivating daily practices of gratitude—reflecting on existing resources, acknowledging progress, and appreciating the contributions of others—one maintains an energy that both sustains personal resilience and attracts external opportunities.

Together, collaboration, generosity, and gratitude form the practical applications of abundance thinking. They transform wealth building from a lonely, competitive endeavor into a connected, expansive process. The paradox again reveals itself: those who give, collaborate, and appreciate often find themselves receiving more than they ever pursued directly. In this way, abundance thinking becomes not only a philosophy but a tangible financial strategy.

5.3 Synchronicity and Opportunity Recognition

If abundance thinking creates the fertile soil, synchronicity and opportunity recognition represent the fruits that emerge from it. Synchronicity, as described by Carl Jung, refers to meaningful coincidences—events that seem random yet align perfectly with inner needs or intentions. In wealth creation, synchronicity often manifests as a chance meeting, an unexpected introduction, or the sudden appearance of a solution at precisely the right moment. While skeptics may dismiss this as luck, psychology offers a different interpretation: the mind, when attuned to patterns and possibilities, becomes more capable of recognizing and seizing opportunities that others overlook.

Intuitive decision-making plays a central role here. The subconscious mind processes far more information than conscious awareness can handle, detecting patterns and connections long before they surface as deliberate reasoning. This is why experienced investors, entrepreneurs, or professionals often describe "gut feelings" that prove accurate.

Intuition is not mystical but the distilled wisdom of accumulated experience operating below the surface of conscious thought. Developing trust in this process requires balancing intuition with analysis. When intuition aligns with evidence, it becomes a powerful accelerator of decision-making, allowing one to act quickly in dynamic environments where hesitation costs opportunity. Cultivating intuition involves reflecting on past decisions, learning to distinguish genuine pattern recognition from emotional impulses, and allowing subconscious insights to complement rather than replace rational evaluation.

The prepared mind principle, often attributed to Louis Pasteur's remark that "chance favors the prepared mind," underscores the fact that opportunities rarely appear to those unready to seize them. Synchronicity is not passive luck but the convergence of external events with internal readiness. Psychological readiness means building the knowledge, skills, and confidence necessary to act decisively when chance arises. An entrepreneur who has studied financing options, built networks, and clarified vision is far more likely to secure investment when unexpectedly introduced to a potential backer. A professional who has developed expertise and authority is more likely to recognize a promotion opportunity when it arises. Preparation primes the brain to notice and interpret signals that others dismiss as irrelevant, transforming coincidence into meaningful connection.

Network serendipity expands this principle into the social realm. Opportunities often travel along lines of relationship, appearing not from strangers but through loose ties—friends of friends, colleagues of colleagues—where diversity of information and perspective is greatest. Positioning oneself in environments rich with potential connections dramatically increases the probability of encountering valuable coincidences. This does not mean endless superficial networking but intentional immersion in communities where collaboration, innovation, and opportunity circulate. By cultivating relationships without rigid expectations, one creates a field in which serendipity thrives. The psychological key is openness: remaining receptive to unexpected introductions, willing to explore unfamiliar paths, and ready to act when the right coincidence appears.

Synchronicity and opportunity recognition together illustrate that wealth is not solely engineered through plans but often emerges through the interplay of preparation and openness. Those who rigidly cling to preconceived paths often miss the subtle cues of chance, while those who remain unprepared cannot capitalize even when fortune knocks. Mastery lies in combining discipline with receptivity, preparing relentlessly while also cultivating the flexibility to pivot when unexpected openings appear.

Ultimately, wealth creation at its highest level is not a battle against scarcity but a dance with abundance, synchronicity, and preparedness. It is about trusting that by serving others, giving generously, practicing gratitude, and remaining open to intuition and coincidence, opportunities will not only appear but multiply. The paradox of wealth attraction continues to unfold here: those who release control, embrace generosity, and prepare themselves diligently often encounter "luck" that seems extraordinary to others but feels natural to them. What outsiders see as coincidence is, in truth, the visible outcome of an inner orientation toward abundance and readiness.

In this light, financial success is not simply the product of tactics or strategies but of psychological alignment. It arises when the mind shifts from scarcity to abundance, from control to openness, from fear to trust. Those who adopt these orientations position themselves not only to recognize opportunities but to magnetize them, transforming coincidence into synchronicity and preparation into prosperity.

Chapter 6: Money Relationships and Social Psychology

The Harvard Grant Study, one of the longest-running longitudinal studies of human development, has made a striking discovery: the single strongest predictor of life satisfaction and long-term success—financial as well as personal—is not intelligence, social class, or even genetics, but the quality of one's relationships. For more than eight decades, researchers followed individuals across their lifespans, and time and again, the findings pointed to the same conclusion: people who cultivated healthy, supportive, and communicative relationships were not only happier but also more financially resilient and prosperous. This may at first seem surprising. After all, we often think of financial outcomes as the product of individual skill, effort, or luck. Yet money does not exist in a vacuum—it flows through the fabric of social life. It shapes marriages, friendships, and professional ties. The ability to navigate financial conversations, set boundaries, and negotiate agreements without corroding trust is one of the most underappreciated skills in wealth building.

6.1 Financial Communication Mastery

If money is among the most common sources of conflict in relationships, it is also one of the most neglected areas of honest dialogue. Couples avoid discussing it for fear of sparking arguments. Friends remain silent about debts or obligations to preserve harmony. Business partners defer tough financial conversations until resentment festers. These avoidance patterns are not signs of weakness but reflections of how emotionally charged money is. It carries connotations of security, status, identity, and even love. To master financial communication is therefore not simply about learning words or techniques—it is about developing the psychological tools to speak openly about one of the most sensitive areas of human life while maintaining trust and connection.

Money conversation skills begin with the recognition that defensiveness often arises not from the numbers themselves but from what those numbers represent. A request to save more may be heard as criticism of spending habits. A suggestion to invest differently may be interpreted as a lack of trust. The first psychological technique for avoiding defensiveness is to frame conversations in terms of shared goals rather than individual shortcomings. Instead of saying, "You spend too much," one might say, "I'd like us to work together to strengthen our financial security so we both feel less stressed." This reframing transforms potential blame into collaboration. Another powerful technique is active listening—reflecting back what the other person has expressed to ensure understanding. By demonstrating that each party's perspective is valued, conversations shift from battles to dialogues.

Timing also matters. Financial discussions held in the heat of frustration are far more likely to spiral into conflict. Psychological research shows that people regulate emotions more effectively when discussions occur in calm, neutral settings. Scheduling conversations, rather than springing them unexpectedly, allows both parties to prepare mentally. The simple act of setting the stage—choosing a quiet time, clarifying intentions, and committing to respectful dialogue—creates an environment where the nervous system feels safe, reducing the likelihood of defensive escalation.

Beyond personal relationships, financial communication mastery extends into professional life through negotiation psychology. Negotiation is not about domination or trickery but about understanding the principles of leverage, reciprocity, and influence. Leverage arises when one recognizes the true value they bring to the table. Often, individuals underestimate their worth, entering negotiations apologetically rather than confidently. By documenting accomplishments, quantifying contributions, and understanding the other party's needs, negotiators build a foundation of strength that naturally commands respect. Reciprocity, the principle that people feel compelled to return favors, can be leveraged ethically in negotiation by offering concessions strategically. For instance, demonstrating flexibility in one area can increase the likelihood of receiving agreement in another. Influence, meanwhile, often operates less through force than through framing. The way a proposal is presented—whether as a gain, a shared benefit, or a solution to a pressing problem—can dramatically shape outcomes.

Negotiation psychology is not confined to boardrooms or contracts. It plays out daily in families and friendships: deciding how to split expenses, determining financial roles in a household, or agreeing on joint purchases. Those who approach these situations with adversarial mindsets often erode trust, but those who approach them with collaborative negotiation techniques strengthen both the financial and emotional fabric of relationships. A well-negotiated agreement is not one where one party "wins" but where both feel respected, understood, and committed to the outcome.

Equally important in financial communication is the ability to set boundaries. Without boundaries, relationships risk becoming entangled in patterns of manipulation, resentment, or dependency. Many people struggle here because financial boundaries are often conflated with rejection or lack of generosity. Yet in truth, clear boundaries preserve relationships by preventing silent bitterness from taking root. Consider the friend who continually borrows money without repayment. Without boundaries, the lender may grow resentful, eroding the friendship. By contrast, a clear boundary—such as refusing to lend but offering non-financial support—protects both the relationship and the individual's financial health.

Boundary setting requires psychological clarity. It involves discerning between generosity that feels aligned and demands that feel exploitative. It also involves communicating limits with firmness and respect. Phrases like, "I'm not able to contribute financially in that way, but I'd be happy to help in another," reinforce that boundaries are not punishments but expressions of self-respect. When boundaries are consistently maintained, relationships adjust. Those who respect them grow closer, appreciating the honesty. Those who reject them reveal dynamics that may have been unhealthy all along. Either outcome is clarifying, strengthening the overall network of relationships.

The mastery of financial communication, negotiation, and boundary setting creates a powerful ripple effect. Couples who communicate openly about money build trust that translates into shared vision. Families who negotiate fairly reduce conflict across generations. Professionals who approach financial discussions with clarity and confidence earn greater respect and compensation. Communities that cultivate healthy financial dialogue foster cooperation, reducing the hidden resentments that fracture trust. At the core of all these outcomes lies the psychology of communication: the ability to discuss money—an emotionally charged topic—without losing connection.

The Harvard Grant Study's conclusion resonates strongly here. Relationships are the primary determinant of life satisfaction, but they are also key determinants of financial resilience. A supportive partner encourages bold but wise decisions. A network built on trust opens doors to opportunities. A family that communicates openly about money avoids destructive cycles of secrecy and conflict. To cultivate financial communication mastery is therefore to cultivate both prosperity and peace. It is to align one's social world with one's financial world so that the two reinforce rather than undermine each other.

As we move deeper into the psychology of money, this insight becomes increasingly clear: wealth is not built in isolation. It is co-created through the conversations, negotiations, and boundaries that shape our relationships. By mastering financial communication, we not only safeguard our financial future but also strengthen the very fabric of connection that makes that future meaningful.

6.2 Wealthy Network Development

The pursuit of wealth is often framed as an individual endeavor, yet history and psychology alike demonstrate that financial success rarely occurs in isolation. Wealth creation tends to flourish in ecosystems where opportunity, trust, and collaboration intersect. These ecosystems are not accidental; they are deliberately cultivated through the intentional development of social capital. Social capital can be thought of as the web of relationships, trust, and goodwill that an individual accumulates over time, which in turn provides access to mentorship, insider knowledge, and opportunities unavailable to those outside the circle. Unlike financial capital, which can be measured on a balance sheet, social capital is intangible yet often more decisive in determining long-term prosperity.

Building social capital begins with genuine curiosity about others and an orientation toward creating value in relationships. The psychology here is critical: people naturally respond to authenticity, and they recoil from manipulation. Strategic relationship cultivation is not about exploiting contacts for personal gain but about establishing bonds of trust that, over time, lead to mutual benefit. Mentorship is a prime example. When an aspiring professional approaches a seasoned expert, the temptation may be to ask for direct opportunities or favors. Yet the wiser approach is to demonstrate respect, eagerness to learn, and a willingness to contribute. Over time, the mentor's investment in guidance often leads organically to opportunities, introductions, and partnerships. This process highlights the paradox of social capital: those who give first, who seek to enrich relationships without immediate return, end up receiving disproportionately more.

This dynamic is captured in the psychology of reciprocity systems. Human beings are wired to balance the scales of giving and receiving. When someone provides value—whether knowledge, encouragement, or tangible help—the recipient feels a natural pull to reciprocate. The key to building powerful networks is to establish consistent patterns of contribution. Offering introductions, sharing insights, celebrating others' successes, or providing thoughtful support may seem small, yet they accumulate as relationship equity. Over time, this equity translates into tangible benefits. Doors are opened, reputations are enhanced, and opportunities are shared. The most successful wealth builders often appear to attract opportunities effortlessly, but behind the appearance lies years of deliberate reciprocity, where giving became the foundation of receiving.

The creation of high-value circles amplifies these principles. Success breeds success not because wealth itself is contagious, but because mindsets, habits, and opportunities flow more readily in groups where excellence is normalized. The psychology behind this is rooted in social proof and identity. When one surrounds oneself with others who think expansively, act decisively, and create abundantly, those traits are reinforced as part of one's own identity. Conversely, remaining in circles dominated by scarcity, complaint, or short-term gratification drags behavior downward. Attracting and maintaining relationships with successful wealth builders requires alignment in values and vision. It is not enough to seek proximity to the wealthy; one must bring value to the circle as well. This may come in the form of specialized skills, fresh perspectives, or simply a reputation for integrity and reliability. Once established within such a circle, opportunities multiply, as collaboration becomes the natural outcome of shared orientation toward growth.

The development of wealthy networks is therefore not opportunism but the intentional cultivation of environments that make prosperity more likely. Social capital, reciprocity, and high-value circles create an upward spiral where each relationship strengthens access to resources and opportunities. The individual ceases to be a solitary wealth builder and becomes part of an ecosystem where growth is collective, sustained, and far more resilient than any one person's effort could be.

6.3 Family Wealth Psychology

While networks and social circles shape opportunities in the broader world, the deepest and most enduring financial influences are often found within the family. Family dynamics around money can either reinforce prosperity or perpetuate cycles of struggle, and these dynamics are carried across generations unless deliberately examined and reshaped. Family wealth psychology addresses how individuals and households can transform inherited scripts into empowering legacies, aligning spouses, and preparing future generations for responsible stewardship.

Generational money patterns often operate invisibly, shaping behavior long before individuals recognize them. A child raised in a household where debt was constant may unconsciously adopt avoidance strategies around money, shying away from financial planning in adulthood. Conversely, a child who witnesses frugality bordering on deprivation may grow up fearing spending, even when resources are abundant. These inherited scripts perpetuate cycles of scarcity, unless they are consciously disrupted. Breaking negative patterns begins with awareness—asking what messages about money were absorbed from parents and grandparents, and evaluating whether those messages serve one's current goals. By reframing inherited beliefs and modeling healthier behaviors, families can create new narratives. For example, rather than instilling fear around debt, parents can teach discernment, differentiating between destructive borrowing and strategic leverage. In doing so, they transform cycles of limitation into cycles of empowerment.

Spousal financial alignment is another cornerstone of family wealth psychology. Money is among the leading sources of conflict in marriages, not because couples inherently disagree about numbers but because money symbolizes values, priorities, and identity. One partner may equate saving with safety, while the other equates spending with freedom. Without alignment, these differences breed tension and resentment. The psychological techniques for creating unity begin with establishing shared goals that transcend individual preferences. By articulating visions of the future—a desired home, travel, retirement security—couples can anchor financial decisions to shared meaning rather than personal impulse. Open communication, where each partner feels heard and respected, is essential. Compromise, too, plays a role, but compromise without shared vision often feels like loss. Alignment transforms compromise into cooperation, as both partners see themselves working toward a common dream.

Wealth transfer psychology addresses one of the most delicate challenges in family finance: how to prepare both givers and receivers for the dynamics of inheritance and gifts. The absence of preparation often leads to conflict, entitlement, or mismanagement. Children who receive wealth without context may squander it or feel burdened by it, while parents who delay conversations about inheritance may leave behind confusion and resentment. Healthy wealth transfer begins with transparency. Parents who discuss their intentions, explain their reasoning, and invite dialogue create clarity and trust. Equally important is preparing heirs psychologically for stewardship. This involves not only financial education but also instilling values of responsibility, gratitude, and contribution. In this way, inheritance ceases to be a source of conflict and becomes a continuation of legacy.

Family wealth psychology is, at its heart, about aligning money with love, legacy, and responsibility. It is about recognizing that financial decisions within families carry emotional weight and generational consequences. By breaking negative patterns, aligning spouses, and preparing heirs, families can transform money from a source of conflict into a tool for unity and continuity. The result is not only stronger households but also stronger legacies, where financial prosperity and emotional resilience are passed forward together.

Chapter 7: The Psychology of Financial Risk Management

Daniel Kahneman, awarded the Nobel Prize for his groundbreaking work in behavioral economics, illuminated one of the most enduring truths about human decision-making: people experience the pain of losses nearly twice as strongly as they experience the joy of equivalent gains. This single psychological tendency explains much about why so many individuals avoid financial risks that could transform their lives, whether those risks involve investing in markets, starting a business, or even negotiating for a higher salary. While risk aversion can serve a protective role, it also creates invisible walls that prevent people from stepping into opportunities. True financial mastery requires not the elimination of fear but the cultivation of intelligent frameworks for understanding, evaluating, and managing risk. When risk is approached with clarity rather than emotion, it ceases to be a barrier and becomes a tool for wealth creation and preservation.

7.1 Intelligent Risk Assessment

The first step toward intelligent risk assessment lies in shifting from possibility-based thinking to probability-based thinking. The human brain is naturally attuned to possibilities, especially negative ones. This makes sense from an evolutionary perspective: our ancestors survived by anticipating worst-case scenarios—whether a predator in the bushes or a sudden famine. But in the financial realm, this instinct often leads to paralysis.

Many people focus obsessively on what could go wrong, even if the probability is vanishingly small. For example, an investor may avoid placing money in a diversified index fund because of the possibility of a market crash, ignoring the much higher probability of steady long-term growth. Similarly, someone might refuse to launch a business for fear of failure, disregarding the probability that the skills gained in the attempt would create new, valuable opportunities even if the first venture faltered.

Shifting to probability thinking means training the mind to weigh outcomes based on expected value rather than emotional salience. Expected value considers both the likelihood of an event and its magnitude. For instance, while a market downturn is always possible, the probability that markets recover and trend upward over decades is historically very high, giving long-term investing a strong expected value. By focusing on probabilities rather than isolated possibilities, individuals can evaluate risks more rationally. Psychological techniques such as scenario planning help here: instead of asking, "What if everything goes wrong?" one asks, "What are the most likely scenarios, and how would each affect me?" This shift reframes risk from a looming threat into a spectrum of outcomes that can be prepared for and managed.

Equally important is distinguishing between risk capacity and risk tolerance. Too often, people conflate these concepts, leading to either reckless exposure or unnecessary conservatism. Risk capacity refers to the objective ability to withstand financial loss. It is determined by concrete factors such as income stability, asset base, time horizon, and existing obligations. A young professional with steady income and decades before retirement has far greater risk capacity than someone approaching retirement with limited savings. Risk tolerance, on the other hand, refers to the subjective comfort with uncertainty—the emotional threshold beyond which anxiety becomes debilitating. Someone may have high capacity but low tolerance, avoiding equities despite the ability to weather volatility. Another may have low capacity but high tolerance, chasing speculative investments despite being unable to afford significant losses.

The psychological mastery of risk involves aligning these two dimensions. When tolerance is lower than capacity, education and gradual exposure to volatility can expand comfort zones, allowing individuals to harness their true potential. When tolerance is higher than capacity, discipline is required to impose guardrails, protecting against overexposure. One practical approach is to segment investments into layers: allocating a portion to safe, stable assets that provide peace of mind, while directing another portion to growth-oriented assets that maximize capacity. This balance ensures that individuals neither undershoot their potential out of fear nor jeopardize their future out of overconfidence.

Insurance psychology represents another critical dimension of intelligent risk management. Insurance, in essence, is the transfer of catastrophic risk from the individual to an institution. Rationally, it exists to protect against events that would be financially devastating: a medical emergency, a house fire, the death of a breadwinner. Yet psychology often distorts how people approach insurance. Fear leads some to over-insure, buying coverage for minor risks that could be absorbed without catastrophe, such as extended warranties or redundant policies. Others, driven by denial or optimism bias, under-insure, leaving themselves vulnerable to events that could erase years of financial progress.

To make rational insurance decisions, individuals must again return to expected value thinking. The purpose of insurance is not to eliminate every inconvenience but to safeguard against ruin. Understanding this distinction requires examining not only the likelihood of events but also their potential magnitude. For example, the probability of a house fire may be small, but the financial devastation it would cause justifies home insurance. The likelihood of a smartphone breaking is higher, but the financial consequence is small enough that insuring it may not be cost-effective. Rational insurance psychology involves distinguishing between risks that threaten comfort and risks that threaten survival, insuring only against the latter.

The challenge lies in resisting the emotional marketing that exploits fear. Insurance companies are well aware of loss aversion and craft messages designed to amplify it. The intelligent investor learns to filter these messages through a rational framework, asking: Does this policy protect me against a risk that could truly derail my financial life? If the answer is no, then the policy may not be necessary. By applying this filter consistently, one develops a disciplined approach to risk transfer, ensuring that resources are not wasted on unnecessary premiums but directed toward meaningful protection.

Together, probability thinking, alignment of risk capacity and tolerance, and rational insurance practices form the foundation of intelligent risk assessment. They transform risk from an amorphous fear into a measurable, manageable component of financial strategy. Rather than avoiding risk altogether—a stance that paradoxically carries its own risks, such as inflation eroding cash savings—individuals learn to embrace it intelligently. They recognize that every meaningful financial gain requires stepping into uncertainty, but that uncertainty can be navigated with clarity, preparation, and balance.

Daniel Kahneman's insight into loss aversion reminds us why this mastery is so essential. Left unchecked, our natural psychology drives us to overemphasize losses, underestimate resilience, and overpay for security. Intelligent risk assessment does not deny these instincts but transcends them, building frameworks that allow rational action even when emotions protest. The result is not only stronger financial outcomes but also greater peace of mind, as individuals learn that risk is not an enemy but an ally when engaged with wisdom.

7.2 Emergency Preparedness Mindset

Financial risk management is not only about evaluating investments and probabilities; it is also about preparing mentally and practically for crises. Emergencies—whether personal, such as illness, job loss, or unexpected expenses, or systemic, such as recessions, pandemics, or geopolitical shocks—are inevitable across a lifetime. What separates those who weather storms successfully from those who collapse under the weight of uncertainty is not luck alone but psychology. The mindset of preparedness provides both confidence and clarity, ensuring that when disruptions arise, panic does not take over.

The psychology of financial security rests on systematic preparation. When individuals build emergency reserves, diversify income sources, and establish contingency plans, they create a buffer that protects not just their bank accounts but their mental health. Knowing that there are resources to draw upon in the event of disruption allows the nervous system to remain calm. Without preparation, even minor crises can feel catastrophic. For instance, a car repair bill might devastate someone with no savings but hardly faze someone who has intentionally created a financial cushion. The security mindset is less about stockpiling endlessly and more about trusting that careful planning provides stability. It fosters confidence by reducing the fear of the unknown, replacing it with assurance that while challenges are inevitable, survival is not in question.

Yet emergencies rarely unfold exactly as expected, which is why adaptive resilience is a crucial psychological trait. Too often, individuals prepare rigidly for one specific scenario, only to be blindsided by a different challenge. A worker may prepare for the possibility of job loss by saving diligently, only to find themselves instead facing inflation that erodes the value of those savings. Adaptive resilience means cultivating the flexibility to pivot strategies as circumstances evolve. Psychologically, this requires reducing attachment to specific outcomes and instead focusing on principles. A resilient mindset asks not, "Did the exact scenario I feared happen?" but rather, "How can I adapt with the tools and resources I have?" This flexibility prevents paralysis when reality diverges from expectation.

Stress testing scenarios provide a practical method for strengthening this resilience. Just as banks test their systems against hypothetical downturns, individuals can mentally rehearse financial challenges. Imagining what steps one would take if income were halved, if markets plunged, or if a medical emergency struck allows the mind to process fear in advance. This psychological rehearsal reduces shock when real crises arrive, enabling clear thinking instead of panic. Importantly, stress testing is not about wallowing in worst-case thinking but about rehearsing adaptive responses. When one has already thought through potential moves, such as cutting discretionary spending, liquidating certain assets, or tapping lines of credit, the brain can act decisively rather than floundering in uncertainty. The result is calm execution rather than chaotic reaction.

An emergency preparedness mindset is therefore a psychological safety net. It acknowledges that crises cannot be avoided but can be anticipated, buffered against, and navigated with resilience. The prepared mind does not eliminate fear but contextualizes it, transforming vague anxieties into specific scenarios with actionable responses. This clarity builds confidence, ensuring that financial storms, while disruptive, do not derail the long-term trajectory of wealth building.

7.3 Calculated Risk Taking

While preparedness safeguards against downside, wealth creation ultimately requires moving toward uncertainty. To grow beyond the confines of security, one must learn the art of calculated risk taking. Unlike reckless gambles, calculated risks are ventures where downside is limited but upside is expansive. The psychology of such risk taking lies in balancing fear with vision, caution with courage, and recognizing that failure itself can be reframed as a necessary step in mastery.

One of the most powerful concepts in this domain is asymmetric bet recognition. An asymmetric bet is one in which potential losses are capped or manageable, while potential gains are disproportionately large. Entrepreneurs, investors, and innovators often thrive by spotting these opportunities. For example, investing a small portion of capital in an early-stage company could mean limited loss if it fails but exponential return if it succeeds. Psychologically, asymmetric bets require training the mind to see beyond the immediate discomfort of uncertainty and to evaluate outcomes across a spectrum of possibilities. Instead of fixating on the chance of loss, the contrarian thinker asks: what is the ratio between the worst case and the best case, and does the upside justify the attempt? By cultivating this lens, individuals can seize opportunities others avoid, compounding advantage over time.

However, few people can leap into risk headfirst without preparation. This is where the psychology of the risk ladder becomes essential. Risk tolerance grows gradually, much like physical endurance. A novice investor who places their life savings into volatile assets is not practicing bravery but recklessness. Instead, building comfort with risk requires incremental exposure. Beginning with small, manageable risks trains the nervous system to tolerate uncertainty while observing that setbacks are rarely fatal. Each successful step expands the comfort zone, enabling progression to larger ventures. Psychologically, this ladder approach transforms risk from something terrifying into something familiar, progressively rewiring the brain to view uncertainty as navigable rather than overwhelming.

Central to calculated risk taking is the reframing of failure. Fear of mistakes paralyzes many would-be wealth builders, leading them to cling to safety even when opportunities abound. Yet failure, when interpreted correctly, is not a dead end but a feedback loop. Every unsuccessful attempt provides data—about strategy, timing, execution, or market dynamics—that refines future choices. The difference between those who stagnate and those who succeed is often not the absence of failure but the interpretation of it. To view failure as shameful is to withdraw from learning. To view it as tuition paid in the school of wealth is to accelerate mastery. Reframing requires conscious effort: instead of asking, "What did this loss say about me?" one asks, "What did this experience teach me about the game I am playing?" Over time, the accumulation of lessons transforms fear into resilience, and resilience into confidence.

Calculated risk taking is therefore not about eliminating doubt but about engaging with it intelligently. It means asking whether potential rewards justify potential costs, expanding tolerance gradually through exposure, and embracing failure as part of the process. The paradox is that by leaning into risk, wealth builders often reduce the danger they feared. This is because familiarity with uncertainty builds psychological resilience, while avoidance leaves fear unchallenged and magnified.

Together, emergency preparedness and calculated risk taking form complementary halves of financial resilience. One safeguards against the inevitability of setbacks; the other propels growth despite uncertainty. The prepared individual can face crises without collapse, while the risk taker can pursue opportunities without paralysis. Both are necessary for lasting wealth. Preparedness without risk leads to stagnation. Risk without preparedness leads to ruin. In balance, they create the psychological foundation for navigating the unpredictable landscape of finance with both confidence and vision.

Chapter 8: Psychological Wealth
Preservation Strategies

Studies of wealthy families consistently highlight a sobering statistic: by the third generation, nearly 90 percent of fortunes have disappeared. This phenomenon, often summarized by the adage "shirtsleeves to shirtsleeves in three generations," reveals that the erosion of wealth is seldom caused by external forces such as taxation, inflation, or markets. Instead, the collapse of prosperity is largely psychological, rooted in how families adapt—or fail to adapt—to money across generations. Patterns of entitlement, overspending, lack of discipline, or complacency slowly dissolve fortunes that once seemed indestructible. Preserving wealth requires far more than legal structures or financial vehicles; it requires cultivating mindsets that sustain prosperity long after the initial creation of it.

8.1 Wealth Maintenance Psychology

At the heart of wealth preservation lies the challenge of managing lifestyle inflation. As income and assets grow, so too do expectations of comfort and luxury. This is not merely a practical issue but a psychological one, driven by the hedonic treadmill— the tendency of humans to quickly adapt to improved circumstances and reset their baseline of satisfaction. A person who once found joy in a modest car may soon feel dissatisfied unless they own a luxury vehicle, not because the first car is inadequate but because the mind adjusts upward. Over time, spending escalates in lockstep with income, leaving little room for saving or reinvestment despite apparent prosperity.

Avoiding this treadmill requires conscious psychological techniques. The first is cultivating awareness of adaptation itself. When individuals recognize that pleasure from new acquisitions fades more quickly than anticipated, they become less susceptible to endless upgrading. Mindful spending—asking whether a purchase truly enhances long-term satisfaction or merely serves as a fleeting boost—creates space between impulse and action. Another strategy is grounding lifestyle choices in values rather than comparisons. Instead of chasing status symbols because peers display them, one can ask whether an expense genuinely enriches family life, personal growth, or meaningful experiences. This shift in perspective preserves enjoyment of wealth without letting it spiral into compulsive consumption.

Another challenge lies in the success trap. When initial goals of financial independence or comfort are achieved, motivation often diminishes. Without the urgency of survival or the excitement of growth, individuals can stagnate, drifting into complacency that leaves wealth unguarded. The psychology here is subtle: success, if not carefully managed, can erode the very drive that produced it. Entrepreneurs who once fought tirelessly to build fortunes may relax too soon, neglecting reinvestment or failing to adapt as industries evolve. Heirs who inherit wealth without experiencing the struggle of creation may take abundance for granted, assuming it will endure regardless of stewardship.

Escaping the success trap requires deliberately maintaining a growth mindset even after milestones are reached. This does not mean rejecting rest or enjoyment but embracing new forms of challenge. For some, this may involve shifting focus from wealth creation to legacy building—supporting philanthropy, funding innovation, or mentoring others. For others, it may mean setting fresh financial goals that stretch beyond comfort zones, such as expanding into new markets or diversifying investments. The key is to preserve curiosity and drive, ensuring that wealth remains dynamic rather than static. The healthiest psychological stance sees wealth not as an endpoint but as a resource for continued growth, whether personal, familial, or societal.

Balancing gratitude with ambition is perhaps the most delicate psychological act of wealth preservation. Gratitude plays a protective role: it anchors individuals in appreciation, reducing the restless craving that drives lifestyle inflation. Grateful individuals enjoy what they have, insulating themselves from the corrosive dissatisfaction of perpetual comparison. Yet gratitude, if not paired with continued vigilance, can tip into complacency. Families who assume that fortune will always remain may neglect discipline, failing to save or manage risk effectively. Thus, preservation requires a dynamic balance: appreciating wealth as a blessing while recognizing that it must be actively safeguarded.

This balance can be nurtured through deliberate practices. Reflecting regularly on the journey that led to prosperity fosters humility, reminding individuals that wealth is fragile and not guaranteed. Teaching children about the sacrifices, risks, and discipline behind financial success creates continuity of values, ensuring they understand that preservation requires responsibility. Simultaneously, structured planning— maintaining budgets, setting investment strategies, and reviewing financial goals—keeps the drive for protection alive. In this way, gratitude coexists with vigilance, producing a mindset that enjoys prosperity without assuming its permanence.

Ultimately, wealth maintenance psychology is about resisting the silent forces that erode fortunes from within. Lifestyle inflation tempts individuals into overspending, the success trap lulls them into complacency, and unchecked gratitude can dull ambition. By countering these patterns with mindful awareness, continued growth orientation, and balanced appreciation, families can sustain wealth across generations. Preservation becomes not a passive inheritance but an active discipline, woven into daily choices and long-term vision.

The fate of most wealthy families illustrates what happens when these psychological dynamics are ignored. The first generation often builds wealth through hard work and sacrifice. The second, raised in comfort, enjoys and expands it but begins to lose touch with the grit that created it. By the third, entitlement and complacency often take hold, and without the psychological tools to counteract these forces, fortunes unravel. Reversing this pattern requires cultivating wealth maintenance as a mindset, not a moment. It is not enough to accumulate; one must continually manage, reassess, and adapt.

Those who succeed in preserving wealth across generations share common traits: they understand the hedonic treadmill and resist constant upgrading, they avoid the success trap by seeking new forms of growth, and they balance gratitude with vigilance. These are not technical skills alone but psychological disciplines, requiring self-awareness, humility, and resilience. By embedding these practices into family culture and personal identity, wealth can endure not just for decades but for centuries, providing security, opportunity, and legacy for those who come after.

8.2 Diversification Psychology

The concept of diversification has been emphasized by investors, economists, and advisors for centuries, but its practice is often undermined not by lack of knowledge but by psychological biases. Concentration risk—relying too heavily on a single income stream, asset, or investment—is alluring because it offers simplicity and the illusion of control. Yet, in reality, it exposes individuals and families to vulnerabilities that can wipe out wealth in an instant. The irony is that many who fall into concentration do so because of past success. An entrepreneur who built a fortune in one industry may assume that their sector will always sustain growth, neglecting the possibility of disruption. An employee with a high-paying job may believe their role or company will provide lifelong stability, ignoring the fragility of careers. These beliefs are reinforced by cognitive biases such as overconfidence and familiarity bias. The brain naturally prefers what it knows, convincing individuals that the future will mirror the past.

To overcome these biases, diversification psychology requires a deliberate reframing of risk. Instead of perceiving diversification as dilution, one must view it as resilience. The key is to embrace the uncomfortable reality that no single source of income or investment is infallible. This does not mean abandoning successful ventures but complementing them with others that respond differently to market forces. By recognizing the mind's tendency to overweight familiar paths, individuals can consciously challenge themselves to consider alternatives, spreading exposure in ways that protect against catastrophic loss. The discipline lies in asking not only, "What has worked for me?"

but also, "What could undermine me if I rely too much on it?" This awareness anchors a healthier relationship to diversification.

Geographic diversification extends this principle beyond sectors into borders. Modern wealth is global, and risks are not confined to domestic markets. Political upheaval, inflation, or regulatory changes can undermine fortunes in one country even while opportunities flourish in another. Yet many individuals remain psychologically tethered to their home regions, preferring to invest and operate where they feel most comfortable. This home bias is deeply ingrained; the familiar feels safer even when objective analysis suggests otherwise. Breaking free from this limitation requires cultivating mental models that view wealth as borderless. Instead of asking, "Where do I live?" one asks, "Where does my money thrive?" The global perspective not only reduces risk but expands opportunity, unlocking access to markets, currencies, and industries unavailable domestically.

Adopting a global mindset does not demand reckless scattering of resources across the world but intentional positioning that acknowledges interconnected risk. For instance, an investor may balance assets between developed and emerging markets, or an entrepreneur may explore partnerships across regions to mitigate reliance on one economy. The psychological challenge lies in embracing uncertainty and difference—trusting that diversity across borders strengthens security rather than dilutes focus. By training the mind to see the world as a mosaic of opportunities rather than a single familiar terrain, geographic diversification becomes less intimidating and more natural.

Time diversification represents yet another dimension, balancing present enjoyment with future security. Human beings are

91

naturally present-biased; the immediate pleasure of spending often outweighs the distant benefits of saving or investing. This short-termism explains why many people fail to accumulate wealth despite sufficient income. To counter this bias, time diversification psychology requires reframing consumption as a distribution problem across life stages. The question shifts from "What do I want now?" to "How do I allocate resources across decades to maximize both present fulfillment and future stability?"

This framework helps individuals resist two extremes: deferring all enjoyment in the name of security or consuming recklessly at the expense of tomorrow. The balance is achieved by anchoring financial decisions in life cycles—understanding that youth, middle age, and retirement each demand different mixes of consumption and preservation. The young professional, for example, may tolerate more investment risk, prioritizing growth while still setting aside experiences that enrich life. Midlife may require a greater emphasis on protection, balancing family needs with future preparation. Later stages demand drawing from accumulated wealth without depleting it prematurely. By adopting a time-diversified mindset, individuals create continuity across their financial lives, avoiding both the regret of missed experiences and the fear of insecurity.

Diversification psychology therefore encompasses more than spreading investments; it is a holistic mindset that acknowledges the limits of certainty. Concentration, while tempting, amplifies vulnerability. Geographic home bias, while comforting, narrows opportunity. Present bias, while natural, undermines long-term stability. By training the mind to embrace diversification across assets, borders, and time, individuals cultivate resilience that ensures wealth not only grows but endures.

8.3 Legacy Building Mindset

Preservation of wealth is not an end in itself. At its highest level, wealth becomes a vehicle for meaning that transcends individual lifetimes. The legacy building mindset shifts the horizon of financial decision-making from decades to generations, anchoring wealth not only in numbers but in purpose, values, and stewardship. Without such a mindset, wealth is vulnerable to the "shirtsleeves to shirtsleeves" cycle, eroding as heirs lack the orientation to maintain it. With it, wealth becomes not a fleeting possession but a lasting foundation.

Intergenerational thinking forms the cornerstone of this mindset. Most financial planning focuses on individual lifespans: retirement, healthcare, estate distribution. But intergenerational wealth demands a longer horizon. It requires asking not only, "How will I live?" but "How will my children and grandchildren thrive?" This extended horizon reshapes decision-making. Investments are evaluated not only for short-term returns but for their ability to sustain growth over decades. Philanthropy is framed not as sporadic giving but as a legacy of impact that continues across generations. Structures such as trusts and family offices may play a role, but the deeper change is psychological: extending the time horizon beyond one's lifetime, embracing the responsibility of planting seeds that will bear fruit long after one is gone.

Values integration is essential for sustaining this commitment. Wealth without values corrodes; it breeds entitlement, conflict, and aimlessness. Families that endure financially are those that align money with mission. This involves articulating the principles that matter most—whether entrepreneurship, education, philanthropy, or resilience—and ensuring that financial decisions reflect them. Teaching children about these values early transforms wealth from mere inheritance into a living mission. Instead of asking, "How do we protect money?" families ask, "How do we use money to advance what we believe in?" This alignment infuses wealth with purpose, creating intrinsic motivation to sustain it.

Stewardship psychology completes the legacy mindset by reframing wealth not as an object to be owned but as a resource to be managed responsibly. Accumulation alone is insufficient; wealth must be maintained, allocated, and distributed wisely. The steward sees themselves not as the ultimate beneficiary but as a caretaker for current and future generations. This psychological orientation tempers ego, encouraging humility and responsibility. It also broadens focus beyond personal consumption to include societal contribution. The steward asks: how can wealth serve not only my family but also my community, my industry, or the world? This perspective transforms wealth from fragile possession into enduring foundation.

The legacy building mindset is therefore a psychological evolution. It begins with extending horizons beyond the self, continues with embedding values into financial life, and culminates in embracing stewardship as an identity. Families that master this mindset not only preserve wealth but amplify its meaning, passing on not just money but culture, resilience, and purpose. They create a narrative that binds generations together, ensuring that wealth does not erode into complacency but flourishes as a living legacy.

Together, diversification psychology and legacy mindset provide the highest guardrails for preservation. Diversification ensures wealth is not lost to unforeseen shocks. Legacy orientation ensures wealth is not lost to internal decay. When combined, they form a psychological fortress, protecting fortunes from both external volatility and internal fragility. In this way, wealth preservation becomes not only a technical exercise but a profound act of vision—protecting resources across time, across borders, and across generations.

Chapter 9: The Psychology of Financial Independence

The rise of the FIRE (Financial Independence, Retire Early) movement has upended long-held assumptions about retirement. For generations, people accepted a standard trajectory: work until sixty-five, then hope for a comfortable retirement sustained by pensions or savings. Yet FIRE adherents have demonstrated that financial freedom is not tethered to age but to psychology. By reframing consumption, savings, and lifestyle choices, they reveal that financial independence can be achieved decades earlier than convention dictates. Their insights are not merely mathematical—although aggressive savings rates and investing strategies play a role—but psychological. They show how shifting definitions of wealth, rethinking the value of time, and cultivating optionality can transform financial planning from a rigid pursuit into a path toward genuine freedom.

9.1 Freedom-Focused Financial Planning

True wealth cannot be reduced to a number on a balance sheet. While conventional planning often emphasizes accumulation— "I need X dollars to retire"—this framing can obscure the deeper purpose of financial independence. The psychological exploration of true wealth asks: what does independence actually mean to me? For some, it is the ability to walk away from a job they dislike. For others, it is the capacity to spend more time with family, pursue creative passions, or contribute to causes they care about. In each case, the meaning of wealth lies not in possession but in liberation—the freedom to design life around values rather than obligations.

This reframing is crucial because accumulation alone can become a trap. Many who chase financial independence as a number discover that the goalpost keeps shifting. Once one million is achieved, the mind demands two million, then three. The hedonic treadmill is not confined to spending; it infects accumulation as well. Freedom-focused planning interrupts this cycle by defining wealth in qualitative rather than purely quantitative terms. A person who earns modestly but lives in alignment with their values, debt-free and secure, may feel more independent than a millionaire trapped in a high-cost lifestyle they secretly resent. Thus, the first step toward freedom is clarity: independence means autonomy over time and choices, not the endless escalation of net worth.

The second cornerstone of this mindset is the time-money trade-off. Every financial decision, whether spending or saving, ultimately reflects an exchange of life energy. Dollars represent hours of work, focus, and effort. Yet most people treat money as an abstraction, forgetting its direct connection to their finite time. Psychological clarity comes from reframing purchases in terms of hours of life required. For example, a $200 gadget is not simply $200; it may represent ten hours of work after taxes. Once spending is translated back into time, decisions become more grounded. Is the object worth ten hours of life? Could those hours be better used in pursuit of something else?

This analysis reshapes consumption, not through deprivation but through awareness. People often discover that many purchases, when framed as chunks of life energy, lose their appeal.

Conversely, spending that aligns with core values—on experiences, education, or relationships—retains or even increases its worth. The time-money lens also highlights the hidden costs of lifestyle inflation. A larger house, fancier car, or luxury subscription is not merely an expense but a tether, requiring more hours of labor to sustain. By seeing spending as a claim on future time, individuals can prioritize freedom over accumulation of possessions, accelerating the path to independence.

Optionality psychology completes the triad of freedom-focused planning. At its core, optionality is the ability to choose—where to live, how to work, whether to retire, when to travel, or which projects to pursue. Wealth that restricts choice is not true wealth but lifestyle imprisonment. This occurs when individuals build expensive obligations—mortgages, leases, recurring costs—that trap them into sustaining high levels of income even when their passions shift. The paradox is that wealth, if mismanaged, can reduce freedom by demanding constant upkeep.

Optionality, by contrast, is cultivated when financial structures expand choices. Liquid assets that can support sabbaticals, diversified investments that generate passive income, or debt-free living that reduces financial pressure all create conditions for flexibility. Psychology plays a central role here because optionality requires resisting the cultural narrative that equates success with accumulation of fixed assets and visible status markers. The wealthy homeowner tied to a mansion in a city they dislike is less free than the modest earner with portable assets who can relocate at will. True independence is measured not by the size of possessions but by the range of available options.

Optionality also provides resilience. Life is unpredictable—careers shift, health changes, opportunities arise unexpectedly. Those who build optionality into their financial design can pivot gracefully, while those locked into rigid lifestyles struggle. A portfolio balanced between growth and liquidity, a career with multiple skills rather than narrow specialization, or relationships across diverse networks all contribute to this flexibility. Psychologically, optionality reduces anxiety because it provides escape valves. Knowing that one can downsize, relocate, or shift work alleviates the fear of being trapped. Independence becomes less about controlling every outcome and more about ensuring that no single outcome dictates life.

When freedom-focused planning integrates these elements—true wealth definition, time-money awareness, and optionality—it transforms financial independence from a distant dream into a living process. It dismantles the myth that independence requires extraordinary income or luck, replacing it with the recognition that mindset and design are decisive. Those who clarify what independence means to them, evaluate spending through the lens of life energy, and cultivate flexibility find themselves freer at far earlier stages of life than those who pursue accumulation blindly.

The FIRE movement illustrates these principles vividly. Its practitioners often achieve independence not by earning astronomical salaries but by questioning assumptions. They reject lifestyle inflation, anchor spending in values, and prioritize optionality. Their psychology emphasizes freedom over conformity, presence over possession. While not everyone desires extreme early retirement, the broader lesson applies universally: financial independence is as much a psychological design as a financial one.

In the end, freedom-focused financial planning is less about retiring from life than retiring from compulsion. It is about replacing obligation with choice, scarcity with sufficiency, and passive acceptance with deliberate design. Those who embrace this psychology discover that independence is not a finish line but a mindset—one that can be practiced daily in the way they earn, spend, save, and live. By aligning money with freedom rather than accumulation, they unlock the truest definition of wealth: the ability to live life on their own terms.

9.2 Minimalist Wealth Strategies

Financial independence often suffers not from too little money but from too many competing desires. Modern consumer culture conditions people to constantly seek more—more possessions, more upgrades, more symbols of success—without ever defining what "enough" truly means. This pursuit becomes a treadmill where satisfaction is always postponed to the next purchase, the next promotion, the next number in an investment account. Minimalist wealth strategies are not about deprivation but about reclaiming clarity, cultivating satisfaction, and channeling resources toward what genuinely enriches life. By mastering the psychology of "enough," shifting toward quality rather than quantity, and prioritizing experiences over possessions, individuals can accelerate both freedom and happiness.

The psychology of enough begins with internal satisfaction signals. These signals are often muted by cultural noise, where advertising and social comparison drown out authentic needs. A person may have sufficient resources to live securely and comfortably, yet still feel inadequate because their lifestyle does not match those around them. This endless comparison fuels consumption without purpose. The antidote is cultivating the inner ability to recognize sufficiency. This involves deliberate reflection on what level of consumption genuinely supports well-being. Journaling about gratitude, conducting "enough audits" of possessions, and clarifying personal values help recalibrate satisfaction signals. When individuals can look at their lives and say, "This is sufficient for me," they gain freedom from the compulsive need for more. Enough becomes not a limitation but liberation—the moment where money no longer controls life, but serves it.

Closely related is the quality versus quantity mindset. Consumer psychology often drives people to equate more with better. Yet research in positive psychology shows that satisfaction per dollar spent is maximized not by acquiring more items but by selecting fewer, higher-quality purchases that align with genuine values. A closet crammed with cheap clothing rarely provides the same joy as a few well-made garments that last for years. A home cluttered with gadgets may feel overwhelming, while a carefully chosen set of tools can bring clarity and function. By adopting the quality-over-quantity lens, individuals not only reduce waste but also extend the longevity of satisfaction. This mindset requires slowing down decision-making, resisting impulse purchases, and asking whether an item will truly add value over time. In doing so, spending shifts from compulsive consumption to intentional investment in well-being.

The final pillar of minimalist wealth strategy is the recognition that experiences yield greater happiness than possessions. Experiences provide emotional resonance, social connection, and memories that grow richer over time. A vacation with loved ones, a concert, or even a simple shared meal continues to deliver joy years after the event, as the memory is revisited and retold. Possessions, by contrast, often fade into the background as novelty wears off. From a psychological perspective, investing in experiences creates compounding happiness, much like compound interest builds wealth. By reallocating spending toward experiences that align with values—travel, education, hobbies, time with family—individuals maximize the return on each dollar, not in financial terms but in quality of life.

Minimalist wealth strategies therefore serve as both a financial accelerator and a psychological stabilizer. By knowing what is enough, focusing on quality, and prioritizing experiences, people spend less without feeling deprived. This lowers the cost of living, increases savings rates, and speeds the path to independence. At the same time, it enriches life in the present, ensuring that freedom is not deferred to some distant future but enjoyed along the way.

9.3 Passive Income Psychology

If minimalist strategies reduce the demands on wealth, passive income expands the supply. Together, they form the two wings of financial independence: lowering the threshold of what is required while increasing the flow of resources available. The psychology of passive income is distinct from that of active earning. It requires shifting from trading time for money to building systems where money flows independent of constant labor. This shift is less technical than psychological, involving a reorientation of how one views assets, time, and scalability.

The foundation lies in asset versus liability thinking. Assets are not defined merely by ownership but by whether they generate positive cash flow. Liabilities, conversely, drain resources even if they appear prestigious. A large home may be socially admired but, if it demands constant upkeep and mortgage payments, it functions as a liability. A modest rental property, by contrast, may look less glamorous but produces steady income, qualifying as an asset. Developing the mental model of categorizing decisions by their cash flow impact rewires thinking. Each purchase is evaluated not by status or desire but by whether it puts money in one's pocket or takes it out. Over time, this binary lens becomes second nature, guiding decisions toward building streams of income rather than drains of expenditure.

Building passive income requires the system-building mindset. Most people are conditioned to equate income with effort: more hours worked equals more money earned. Passive income challenges this equation by emphasizing systems that operate independently once established. These systems may take the form of investments, intellectual property, automated businesses, or technology platforms. The psychological hurdle is the upfront cost of effort without immediate reward. Writing a book, building a course, or establishing an investment portfolio may take months or years before yielding returns. Many abandon the process because they crave immediate feedback. The system-building mindset, however, accepts delayed gratification, understanding that the payoff arrives later but continues indefinitely. It is a shift from sprinting to marathon running, requiring patience, consistency, and trust in compounding processes.

Scalability recognition is the final psychological frontier of passive income. Not all ventures grow equally. Some opportunities increase income linearly with effort, while others expand exponentially. A consultant billing by the hour, no matter how skilled, remains capped by time. By contrast, an online platform, a well-managed real estate portfolio, or a business built on technology can grow income without proportional increases in work. The challenge lies in training the mind to recognize scalable opportunities and to differentiate them from those that consume more effort with little increase in reward. Scalability is not only about income potential but about freedom: scalable ventures provide flexibility, allowing individuals to design lives around purpose rather than perpetual labor.

Passive income psychology therefore redefines wealth creation. It is not about abandoning work altogether but about transforming work into systems that endure. By categorizing decisions through the asset-liability lens, embracing system-building with patience, and seeking scalability, individuals shift from dependence on wages to autonomy through ownership. The psychological benefits are profound. Anxiety diminishes as reliance on a single income source fades. Confidence grows as multiple streams provide resilience. Most importantly, freedom expands, as time is liberated for pursuits beyond survival.

When combined with minimalist wealth strategies, passive income creates a powerful synergy. Lower costs reduce the threshold of what is required, while systems of income expand what is available. Together, they accelerate the path to independence, proving that financial freedom is not reserved for the exceptionally wealthy but attainable for those who master both consumption and income psychology. True independence, then, emerges not from chasing numbers endlessly but from aligning money with freedom, choice, and meaning.

Chapter 10: Advanced Wealth Psychology Integration

Psychological research into the lives of ultra-high-net-worth individuals offers a paradoxical insight: beyond approximately ten million dollars, wealth provides sharply diminishing returns on happiness unless it is tied to meaning, contribution, and personal growth. This finding disrupts the common assumption that more money automatically equals more fulfillment. Once basic needs, security, and even luxury are abundantly covered, the pursuit of additional wealth no longer produces proportional joy. Instead, it often leaves individuals disoriented, searching for purpose beyond accumulation. The key to sustaining both prosperity and well-being lies not in chasing ever-larger numbers but in integrating wealth with identity, values, and meaning. Without such integration, even great fortunes risk becoming hollow trophies.

10.1 Wealth and Identity Integration

The integration of wealth and identity begins with authentic wealth expression. For many, financial success can create a disconnect between inner values and outer life. They may accumulate wealth by conforming to external expectations—choosing careers, investments, or lifestyles that reflect societal standards rather than personal truths. Yet when the outer display of wealth does not match the inner self, dissatisfaction and emptiness follow. Authentic wealth expression requires aligning financial decisions with personal values and genuine self-expression. For some, this might mean channeling resources into artistic pursuits, philanthropy, or community development. For others, it could involve cultivating a lifestyle that reflects simplicity, sustainability, or adventure rather than status symbols.

Authenticity in wealth expression often demands courage. Social environments exert powerful pressures to conform: driving certain cars, living in certain neighborhoods, sending children to certain schools. Succumbing to these pressures may produce fleeting validation but not lasting fulfillment. The individual who dares to define wealth in their own terms—who invests in what resonates deeply, even if unconventional—experiences harmony between money and identity. In this sense, wealth ceases to be an external marker and becomes a medium of self-expression. The person is no longer living someone else's script but writing their own story with resources that amplify rather than distort their values.

Closely tied to authenticity is the psychology of meaning-making. Wealth accumulation, if pursued only as a game of numbers, eventually loses its motivational power. Once comfort and luxury are secured, the drive for more can feel arbitrary, leading to boredom, aimlessness, or destructive overindulgence. What sustains motivation through challenges is the connection of wealth to larger purposes. Meaning transforms wealth from an end into a tool, from static possession into dynamic contribution. This may take the form of philanthropy, entrepreneurship with social impact, or the creation of legacies that outlast the individual.

Meaning-making psychology is not confined to grand gestures. Even small acts of aligning wealth with purpose—supporting causes one cares about, funding education for the next generation, or creating opportunities for employees—infuse financial pursuits with vitality. Research shows that people who link their work and wealth to causes greater than themselves experience higher resilience, lower stress, and greater satisfaction. The mind, when tethered to purpose, interprets obstacles not as meaningless frustrations but as steps on a larger journey. Wealth building thus becomes not a treadmill but a path of contribution, with each milestone reinforcing a sense of significance.

Identity flexibility represents the final dimension of integration. Wealth, especially when substantial, changes social and financial environments dramatically. Individuals may find themselves in circles of influence they never previously imagined, facing new expectations, opportunities, and challenges. The danger is either clinging rigidly to past identities, creating tension in new contexts, or over-adapting to external pressures, losing core authenticity. Identity flexibility is the capacity to adapt to new realities without abandoning the essence of who one is.

This flexibility allows the wealthy individual to navigate transitions gracefully. For example, moving from middle-class roots into affluence can strain relationships if one feels compelled either to flaunt or to hide new circumstances. With flexibility, the individual maintains connection to old networks while also engaging comfortably with new ones, preserving continuity of self. In professional settings, flexibility enables leaders to shift from the role of operator to steward, from hands-on control to strategic vision, without perceiving these shifts as threats to identity. Psychologically, it is the ability to say, "I remain myself even as my context changes."

At its highest level, identity flexibility enables individuals to resist the corrosive isolation that sometimes accompanies wealth. Many ultra-high-net-worth individuals report loneliness, as they feel alienated from both old friends and new peers. By maintaining a flexible identity, one avoids such disconnection, preserving authenticity while adapting to broader circles. This adaptability also guards against the trap of equating self-worth with net worth. When identity is grounded in values and meaning rather than solely in money, changes in financial fortune do not destabilize the core sense of self.

The integration of wealth and identity is therefore not optional but essential. Without authenticity, wealth feels hollow. Without meaning, wealth feels aimless. Without flexibility, wealth feels isolating. With these elements, however, wealth becomes a platform for expression, growth, and contribution. The individual is no longer merely wealthy but truly independent—able to live, give, and adapt with integrity.

This advanced psychological integration explains why additional millions do not automatically produce more happiness. Once survival and comfort are secured, the mind craves coherence, significance, and adaptability. Wealth, at this stage, is no longer about security but about self. The greatest fortunes that endure across generations are those where money is integrated seamlessly with identity—where financial structures, family cultures, and personal choices reflect authentic values, larger meaning, and flexible adaptation.

Ultimately, wealth and identity integration is the difference between fortune as burden and fortune as blessing. Those who master it discover that money, rather than dictating who they are, amplifies who they already are at their core. Those who neglect it risk losing both wealth and self, consumed by pressures, emptiness, or rigid conformity. Advanced wealth psychology thus demands this integration as its foundation, ensuring that prosperity remains not only intact but fulfilling, both for the individual and for the generations to come.

10.2 Transcendent Wealth Applications

Once wealth reaches a certain threshold, the question is no longer "How do I get more?" but "What do I do with what I have?" At this level, money ceases to be primarily about security or comfort and becomes a medium for influence, impact, and expression. Many ultra-high-net-worth individuals discover that without transcendent applications, wealth turns into a hollow accumulation, providing little beyond fleeting pleasures. The psychology of transcendent wealth reframes money not as an end but as a tool for advancing causes, shaping legacies, and reinforcing a sense of meaning that extends beyond the self.

Impact investing has emerged as one of the clearest illustrations of this shift. Unlike traditional investing, which focuses solely on financial return, impact investing seeks to generate profit while simultaneously producing measurable social or environmental benefits. The psychology behind this approach is grounded in the desire for coherence between values and capital. Investors realize that when money is deployed purely for gain, it can inadvertently support industries or practices misaligned with their ethics. This cognitive dissonance erodes satisfaction, as one part of the self pursues profit while another feels complicit in harm. Impact investing resolves this tension by uniting financial growth with positive outcomes. The investor not only receives returns but also experiences purpose in knowing their capital advances renewable energy, affordable housing, healthcare, or education. The returns, therefore, are doubled: monetary profit combined with psychological fulfillment.

The philanthropic mindset represents a parallel pathway to transcendent wealth. Many assume giving diminishes resources, but strategic generosity often enhances wealth in surprising ways. Psychologically, philanthropy fosters abundance thinking, reinforcing the belief that resources are sufficient to share. This mindset reduces fear and scarcity, replacing them with confidence and resilience. Moreover, giving deepens networks of trust and influence, as generosity attracts collaboration and respect. Historically, great fortunes have endured not only through investment but through philanthropy that built institutions, shaped communities, and left legacies. The wealthy individual who embraces philanthropy does not simply spend; they invest in goodwill, reputation, and impact, all of which compound in ways money alone cannot.

Importantly, philanthropy is most effective when strategic rather than sporadic. Thoughtful giving aligns with long-term missions, ensuring that resources are directed toward causes that reflect core values and produce lasting outcomes. This alignment avoids the psychological trap of guilt-driven giving, which offers momentary relief but little sustained satisfaction. Instead, philanthropy becomes a deliberate expression of identity and purpose, enriching both giver and receiver.

Underlying both impact investing and philanthropy is the broader wealth-as-tool psychology. When wealth is perceived as an end in itself, it often breeds anxiety, entitlement, or emptiness. When reframed as a tool, wealth regains perspective—it becomes a means to achieve goals, support growth, and advance values. This mindset dissolves the illusion that money alone confers worth or meaning. Instead, it anchors financial decisions in a deeper narrative: money serves life, not the other way around. The healthy relationship with wealth sees it as dynamic, flexible, and subordinate to purpose. This perspective not only fosters greater fulfillment but also reduces destructive behaviors like overconsumption, reckless speculation, or hoarding. By understanding wealth as a tool, individuals liberate themselves from its control and channel it toward higher ends.

In sum, transcendent wealth applications transform prosperity into a living force for meaning. Impact investing unites profit with purpose, philanthropy extends legacy through generosity, and wealth-as-tool psychology reframes money as servant rather than master. Together, these orientations ensure that wealth, beyond comfort and security, remains vibrant, purposeful, and deeply fulfilling.

10.3 Continuous Growth Psychology

Even with transcendence achieved, another challenge emerges: how to sustain vitality and growth when financial success is already secured. Many individuals, upon reaching high levels of wealth, face stagnation, boredom, or disorientation. Without a growth orientation, wealth becomes static, and the individual risks slipping into complacency or decline. Continuous growth psychology addresses this challenge by cultivating mindsets that preserve curiosity, innovation, and wisdom, ensuring that prosperity remains a catalyst for personal and collective evolution rather than a plateau.

At the foundation lies the mastery mindset. True masters in any field—whether art, science, or business—maintain a beginner's mind, approaching even familiar subjects with curiosity and humility. In wealth psychology, the mastery mindset prevents individuals from becoming trapped by their own success. Instead of assuming that past methods guarantee future results, they remain students of markets, technologies, and human behavior. This orientation sustains motivation, because growth becomes about deepening understanding rather than merely expanding accumulation. Wealth is no longer a final achievement but a platform for perpetual learning. The wealthy individual who embraces mastery sees every new challenge as an opportunity to refine skill, deepen wisdom, and expand capacity, avoiding the trap of arrogance that often undermines enduring success.

Innovation psychology builds on this foundation by emphasizing openness to new opportunities and strategies as economies and markets evolve. History is replete with fortunes lost because wealth holders clung rigidly to old paradigms. Industries shift, technologies disrupt, and social patterns evolve. The individual who resists innovation becomes vulnerable, while the one who embraces it adapts and thrives. Innovation psychology requires more than technical awareness; it demands a mindset that treats change as opportunity rather than threat. This psychological flexibility allows wealth holders to pivot investments, launch new ventures, or support emerging fields without fear of the unknown. Curiosity replaces rigidity, ensuring that prosperity remains aligned with evolving realities.

Wisdom integration represents the highest expression of continuous growth. Financial intelligence alone is insufficient for holistic success; it must be balanced with emotional and spiritual intelligence. Emotional intelligence ensures that wealth does not isolate but enriches relationships. It fosters empathy, communication, and the ability to navigate complex interpersonal dynamics. Spiritual intelligence provides perspective, reminding individuals that money is temporary, while meaning, contribution, and growth endure. Together, these intelligences temper ambition with humility, power with compassion, and success with responsibility. Wisdom integration ensures that continuous growth is not merely financial but holistic, encompassing all dimensions of human flourishing.

Continuous growth psychology transforms wealth from static possession into dynamic evolution. It prevents the stagnation that often undermines great fortunes, sustaining curiosity, adaptability, and balance. The mastery mindset keeps individuals humble and motivated. Innovation psychology keeps them responsive and forward-looking. Wisdom integration ensures that their growth enriches not only themselves but their families, communities, and the broader world.

At its core, continuous growth psychology reminds us that the journey does not end with financial success. In fact, that is where the deeper journey begins. Wealth, when integrated with identity, transcended into purpose, and sustained through growth, becomes more than prosperity—it becomes a vehicle for lifelong learning, contribution, and wisdom. The individual who embraces this psychology discovers that the true reward of wealth is not accumulation but transformation, both of self and of the world they touch.

Conclusion: Integrating Psychology and Finance for Lasting Wealth

We have now arrived at the closing chapter of a journey that has taken us from the roots of unconscious money scripts to the heights of legacy building and transcendent wealth. Along the way, one truth has become clear: wealth is never just about numbers. It is about the mind that directs those numbers, the stories we tell ourselves, and the values we choose to embody. Money reflects our fears and our hopes, our identities and our relationships, our capacity for discipline and our hunger for meaning. Without psychological awareness, fortunes can vanish, cycles of scarcity repeat, and opportunities pass by unseen. With awareness, however, financial strategies become more than mechanical steps—they become instruments of freedom, empowerment, and fulfillment.

Traditional financial advice often fails because it assumes that knowledge is enough. Save, invest, avoid debt, diversify—these principles are sound, but millions know them and still struggle. The missing piece has always been psychology. We act not from cold logic but from emotional scripts, cultural conditioning, and cognitive biases. We sabotage savings because spending soothes stress. We avoid investments because fear magnifies potential losses. We tie self-worth to possessions and then wonder why happiness fades. The power of this book lies in exposing these patterns and offering tools to transcend them. When psychology aligns with practice, behavior changes naturally, and financial growth follows as a byproduct of clarity and discipline.

The journey began with the Wealth Mindset Matrix, showing how inherited beliefs, cultural programming, and emotional anchoring shape financial ceilings. It revealed the necessity of transitioning from scarcity to abundance, of adopting an identity consistent with wealth, and of cultivating environments that reinforce growth. From there, we explored the neuroscience of financial decision-making, discovering how dopamine, biases, and emotional regulation dictate behavior in markets and daily life. By understanding these forces, we learned to create buffers, filters, and systems that protect against impulsivity and anchor us to long-term vision.

Income expansion psychology taught us that breaking ceilings requires not only skill but courage—the courage to negotiate, to recognize value, to reframe imposter syndrome, and to step into growth. We saw how careers accelerate when skills are stacked, networks cultivated, and authority established, and how entrepreneurship flourishes when risk is calibrated, vision sustained, and scale embraced.

Investment psychology revealed that markets are mirrors of collective emotion, rewarding those who resist herd behavior, detach from media-driven hysteria, and build confidence in contrarian conviction. Long-term wealth emerges not from prediction but from patience, diversification, and behavioral discipline. Through portfolio psychology, we learned how to buffer emotional volatility, automate decisions, and interpret performance realistically, preventing overconfidence on one side and helplessness on the other.

The paradox of wealth attraction showed that money flows most abundantly to those who stop chasing it directly. Service, passion, and flow create disproportionate rewards. Abundance thinking transforms wealth from competition into collaboration, with generosity and gratitude acting as accelerators rather than costs. Synchronicity reminded us that luck favors the prepared, and that openness, intuition, and networks often create opportunities invisible to those locked in rigidity.

We then turned to the psychology of resilience and risk. Kahneman's research on loss aversion explained why we so often flee opportunities, and intelligent risk assessment gave us tools to separate capacity from tolerance, to distinguish probability from possibility, and to insure wisely against ruin without wasting resources. Preparedness provided psychological safety during crises, while calculated risk-taking reframed failure as tuition for success.

Preservation demanded its own psychology: resisting lifestyle inflation, maintaining motivation beyond the first taste of success, and balancing gratitude with vigilance. Diversification across sectors, geographies, and time ensured resilience, while legacy building anchored wealth in values and stewardship, extending horizons beyond individual lifetimes.

Finally, integration elevated wealth from security to transcendence. At advanced stages, prosperity ceases to provide happiness unless it is connected to identity, meaning, and continuous growth. Authentic expression ensures that money amplifies who we are rather than distorts us. Purposeful use of wealth—through impact investing, philanthropy, and contribution—turns accumulation into legacy. Continuous growth ensures that success remains vibrant, with mastery, innovation, and wisdom guiding the way.

The thread that runs through all these stages is alignment. When beliefs, values, and practices align, wealth ceases to be a struggle. It becomes a natural extension of clarity. Scarcity gives way to sufficiency. Fear yields to resilience. Greed transforms into service. Money ceases to enslave and begins to liberate.

Yet the work is not theoretical alone. The concepts explored here culminate in practical transformation. This book does not end with reflection but with an invitation to action. The final section, the 90-day plan, provides a structured path to put psychology into practice, translating insights into measurable results. By applying these tools daily—challenging money scripts, reframing risk, aligning identity, building systems, and cultivating gratitude— readers will begin to see both internal and external shifts. Habits will change, opportunities will appear, and the sense of control over one's financial life will expand.

In the end, the paradox Carl Rogers described remains the key. Only by accepting the money stories we inherited—our fears, our mistakes, our conditioning—can we begin to change them. Wealth does not require perfection, but it does require awareness. Once awareness is cultivated, every choice becomes an opportunity to align money with meaning, to turn numbers into freedom, and to transform wealth into a life lived on purpose.

This book closes, then, not with an endpoint but with a threshold. You now hold both the knowledge and the psychological keys to lasting prosperity. The path ahead will not be free of challenges, but with resilience, clarity, and purpose, those challenges become the very crucibles that shape wisdom. Financial independence, wealth preservation, and legacy creation are not reserved for a select few. They are the birthright of those who choose to align mind and money, psychology and practice, self and purpose. The tools are here. The journey is yours to begin.

www.ingramcontent.com/pod-product-compliance
Lightning Source LLC
Chambersburg PA
CBHW061829220326
41599CB00027B/5236